1978

# PEOPLES OF THE EARTH

volume **1** Australia and Melanesia (including New Guinea)

volume **2** Africa from the Sahara to the Zambesi

volume **3** Europe (including USSR west of the Urals)

volume **4** Mexico and Central America

volume **5** Islands of the Atlantic (including the Caribbean)

volume **6** Amazonia, Orinoco and pampas

volume **7** Andes

volume **8** The Pacific – Polynesia and Micronesia

volume **9** Southern Africa and Madagascar

volume **10** Indonesia, Philippines and Malaysia

volume **11** South-East Asia

volume **12** The Indian subcontinent (including Ceylon)

volume **13** China (including Tibet), Japan and Korea

volume **14** USSR east of the Urals

volume **15** Western and central Asia

volume **16** The Arctic

volume **17** The Arab World

volume **18** North America

volume **19** Man the craftsman

volume **20** The Future of Mankind. General Index

# Man the Craftsman

volume nineteen

THE DANBURY PRESS

(Preceding page) Not only
practicality but art and
instinct for symmetry and
grace direct this Ethiopian
villager as he weaves the
reeds and vines of his
forage hut's roof. Stakes
driven into the ground hold
the circular 'skeleton' at
full stretch while he weaves
the reeds in from the inside.
The completed roof will be
inverted and secured to the
walls of the hut.

The DANBURY PRESS
a division of GROLIER ENTERPRISES INC.
Publisher
ROBERT B. CLARKE

© 1973 Europa Verlag

The series has been created by Tom Stacey Ltd.
All rights reserved. No part of this publication
may be reproduced, stored in a retrieval system,
or transmitted in any form or by any means, electronic,
mechanical, photographic or otherwise without the prior
permission of the copyright owner.

Library of Congress Catalog Card No. 72 85614

Printed in Italy by
Arnoldo Mondadori Editore, Verona

# Contents

*Supervisory Editor of the Series:*
## Professor Sir Edward Evans-Pritchard,
Fellow of All Souls, Professor of Social Anthropology, University of Oxford, 1946-1970, Chevalier de la Légion d'Honneur

*Volume Editor:*
## Shelagh Weir,
Assistant Keeper, Museum of Mankind, British Museum, author of *Palestinian Embroidery* etc

8–11    **Man the craftsman**
Dr Michael Rowlands, Lecturer in the Department of Anthropology, University College London

12–13    **Maps**

14–29    **Man the builder**
B A L Cranstone, Deputy Keeper, Museum of Mankind, British Museum, author of *Melanesia*

30–43    **Man the home-maker**
Keith Nicklin, Research Associate, Nigerian National Museum, Lagos

44–57    **Man the food-getter**
Howard Morphy, M Phil, Department of Anthropology and Prehistory, Australian National University

58–71    **Man attired**
Dale Idiens, Assistant Keeper, Ethnography Department, Royal Scottish Museum, and Jennifer M Scarce, Assistant Keeper, Oriental Department, Royal Scottish Museum

72–85    **Man the music-maker**
Jean Jenkins, Assistant Curator, Horniman Museum

86–99    **Man the traveler**
Keith Nicklin, Research Associate, Nigerian National Museum, Lagos

100–113    **Man the fighter, man the hunter**
Dr Nicholas David, Lecturer in the Department of Anthropology, University College London

114–141    **Man the artist**
Philip Stevens, Department of Anthropology, University College London

142–144    **Mud telephones and plastic gods: culture contact**
Marilyn Hammersley-Houlberg, Lecturer in African Art and History, University of Chicago

STAFF CREDITS
Editorial Director **Tom Stacey**

Picture Director **Alexander Low**
Executive Editor **Katherine Ivens**
Art Director **Tom Deas**
Assistant Editor **Elisabeth Meakin**
Project Co-ordinator **Anne Harrison**
Research **Cheryl Moyer**

Specialist Picture Research **Emma Stacey**
Picture Research **Claire Baines/Elly Beintema/**
**Jeanne Griffiths/Carolyn Keay/Diana Eggitt/**
Editorial Assistants **Richard Carlisle/Rosamund Ellis/**
**Mira Bar-Hillel/Susan Rutherford/Pamela Tubby**
Editorial Secretary **Caroline Silverman**
Design Assistants **Rick Fawcett/Susan Forster/**
**Venetia Greville-Bell/Richard Kelly**
Cartography **Ron Hayward**
Illustrations **Hussein Abo/Clare Brooks/**
**David Godfrey/Roy Hamilton/**
**Wendy Jones/Richard Phipps/Barry Thorpe**

Production **Roger Multon**
Production Editor **Vanessa Charles**

The publishers gratefully acknowledge help from
the following

Museum of Mankind, British Museum, Pitt-Rivers Museum, Musée de
l'Homme, Hamburg Museum, National Trust, Sotheby & Co, Henry
Michael, Mark Edwards, Megan Watts, Alice Mertens, National
Geographic, Horniman Museum, National Gallery, Tate Gallery,
Meyrich Neilson of Tetbury.

PICTURE CREDITS
Cover – **Eigi Miyazawa** (Transworld). **Clinton Bailey** 68 cl. **A. Baum**
(Rapho, New York) 78 bl. **Marc and Evelyne Bernheim** (Woodfin
Camp) 126 cl. **Romano Cagnoni** 96 cr. **Camera Press** 23 br, 97 cr.
**Franklin Cardy** tr. **Peter Carmichael** (C.S.M. Pictures) 54 bl, 96 tl,
106 tl, 108 bl, 112 bl, 134 br. **Cooper-Bridgeman Library** 100, 132 tr.
**E. C. Cranstone** (Axel Poignant) 140 cr. **Derek Davies** 71 cr. **Tamara
Dragazde** 50 tr. **Victor Englebert** 22 tl, 24 cl, 70 tl. **Eriako** (Woodfin
Camp) 109 cr. **Marchel Gompa** 26 cr. **Sonia Halliday** 50 cl. **Robert
Harding Associates** 23 bl, 29 br. **David Harris** 138 cl. **Michael Heron**
43 tl, 129 cl. From the John Hillelson Agency – **Ian Berry** 76-77, 135 tr,
**Dan Budnick** 90-91, **Georg Gerster** 2-3, 20-21, 52 tl, 124-125, 134 cl.
Magnum from the John Hillelson Agency – **Cornell Capa**, 48-49, **A. de
Andrade** 104-105, **Burt Glinn** 62-63, **George Rodger** 34-35, **Marilyn
Silverstone** 121 cl. **The John Hillelson Collection** – 95 cr. **Michael
Hobart** 41 cl, 136-137. **Michael Holford** 129 tr. **Tony
Howarth** (Daily Telegraph) 111 tr, 123 tr. **Jean Jenkins** 79 cr, 80 cl,
81 cr, 83 cl, 84 cl, 85 cr. **Philip Jones Griffiths** 51 cl, 69 tl, 92 cr, 120 cr.
**Romi Khosla** 68 cr. **A. Kupsch** 117. **E. J. Lindgren** 82 br. **Alexander Low**
16, 23 tl, 51 tr, 64 tl, 65 br, 71 cr, 73, 74, 86, 93 cr, 97 cl, 127 tl & cr,
130-131. **John Marmaras** 37 cr. **G. Mary-Rousselière** 53 bl, 67 bl. **John
Massey- Stewart** 54 tr, 138 tr & cr. **Steve McCutcheon** 39 cl. **B. Mertens**
141 cl. **R. Michaud** (Rapho, Paris) 92 tl. **Tchekov Minosa** 30, 103.
**M. de Montmollin** 64 cr. **D. Moore** (Transworld) 14-15, 19, 28 tr. **Tony
Morrison** 41 bl. **Brian Moser** 57 cl, 81 tl, 99 bl, 109 bl, 113 cl. **Horst
Munzig** (Susan Griggs) 98 tl. **R. Murray-Willis** 114. **Erhard Otto** 85 cl.
**Axel Poignant** 24 br, 33, 38 tr, 42 cr, 52 cr, 56 tr, 66 tr, 69 cr, 70 cr, 80 tr,
84 tr, 89, 94 cr, 98 cr, 108 cr, 112 cr, 122 cr, 128 cr. **Carl Purcell** (Trans-
world) 94 cl. **John Picton** 128 bl. **Paul Popper** 141 cr. **Leni Riefenstahl**
61. **M. St. Maur Sheil** (Susan Griggs) 42 bl. **A. Selby** (Louis Mercier)
67 cr. **André Singer** 50 bl, 64 bl. **W. Swaan** (Camera Press) 55 cr.
**Shostal Associates** 135 tl. **Hermann Schlenker** 110 tl. **Emil Schulthess**
(Black Star, New York & Transworld) 39 cr, 44, 53 cr, 57 cr. **R.
Sheridan** 58, **Leif Skoogfas** (Camera Press) 107 cr. **Sean Sprague** 25 cr.
**Philip Stevens** 38 cl. **Bill Strode** (Black Star, New York) 29 tl. **D.
Taylor** 25 bl. **Tiofoto** 99 cr. **Wendy Watriss** (Susan Griggs) 26 tl, 28 cl,
66 cl. **Shelagh Weir** 36 cl, 79 cl. **Adam Woolfitt** (Susan Griggs) 25 tl,
121 tr, **B. Wright** 40 tl. **E. Zalka** 132 tl.
Key: t=top c=center b=bottom r=right l=left

**Peoples of the Earth, volumes one to twenty**

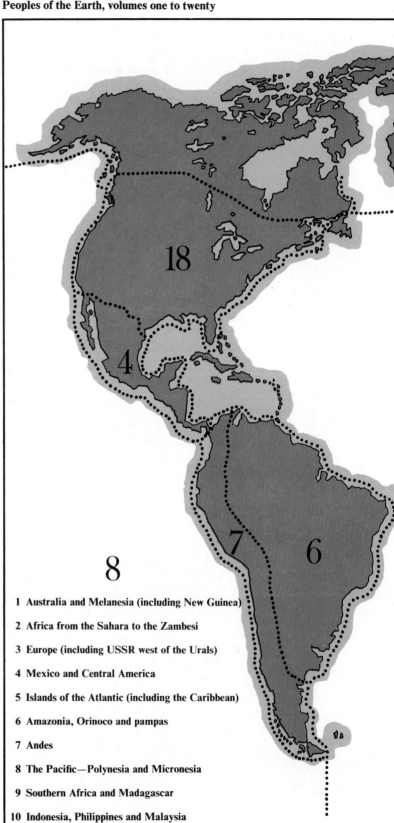

1 **Australia and Melanesia** (including New Guinea)

2 **Africa from the Sahara to the Zambesi**

3 **Europe** (including USSR west of the Urals)

4 **Mexico and Central America**

5 **Islands of the Atlantic** (including the Caribbean)

6 **Amazonia, Orinoco and pampas**

7 **Andes**

8 **The Pacific—Polynesia and Micronesia**

9 **Southern Africa and Madagascar**

10 **Indonesia, Philippines and Malaysia**

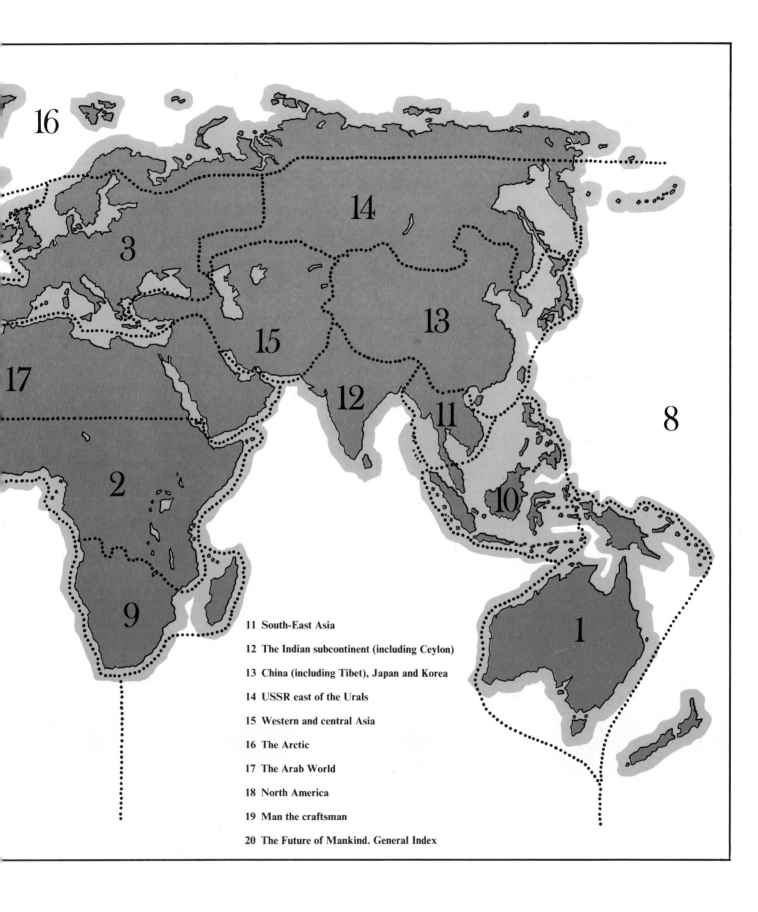

11 South-East Asia

12 The Indian subcontinent (including Ceylon)

13 China (including Tibet), Japan and Korea

14 USSR east of the Urals

15 Western and central Asia

16 The Arctic

17 The Arab World

18 North America

19 Man the craftsman

20 The Future of Mankind. General Index

# Man the craftsman

All human societies have to satisfy the biological needs of their members. Man is an animal species, and like any animal has needs for food and shelter, protection and communication. These needs have to be satisfied by the resources he can find in his local physical environment. However, like any other animal species, man has lived and proliferated in a physical world of tremendous variability where there are extremes of climate, vegetation, soil and topography. The materials necessary for his survival do not always occur in the quantity and forms that are most convenient for him to exploit. Most animal populations overcome this variability by specialization. They adapt biologically – teeth, digestive system, density and color of coat, body weight – to a given range of physical and biological factors in their environment. They learn to exploit this environment effectively, maintaining the reproduction and survival of their species. And so most animal species are limited to particular ecological ranges. Man is exceptional among all animal species in the range of environments to which he has learnt to adapt.

Man has developed a non-biological form of adaptation called culture, which enables him to live practically anywhere on the face of the earth – ranging from equatorial forest to semi-arid desert to temperate woodlands to arctic wastes. In contrast, even man's closest relatives, the anthropoid apes, are limited to the tropical and sub-tropical regions of the world and lack man's capacity to extend their range of habitat.

Because of this the term 'man the tool-maker' has a common use for distinguishing human adaptation from that found for other animal species. As a definition, it is not in fact strictly accurate, since many other animals are known to use tools to supplement their ability to exploit their physical environment. Chimpanzees, for example, have been observed to shape twigs and stalks for extracting ants from their nests and to use leaves as 'cups' with which to drink water. However, it can still be said that it is only man who has developed technology to a complexity whereby the species has extended its environmental range – and is totally dependent upon this technology for its survival. The other distinctive feature is man's use of language for the cultural transmission of information so that such techniques and skills can be handed on from generation to generation. This technological complexity is cumulative in the sense that such techniques and skills were not suddenly acquired but have been added to over thousands of years. If some disaster stripped a human society of its technology not only would it be unlikely to survive but – if it did survive – it would take many generations to rediscover or re-invent a similar system. An important aspect of archaeology is therefore the recording and explanation of human technological progress, and in particular, the general trend for human societies to have extracted more energy from resources that were previously exploited.

Unfortunately no human society lives in a 'Garden of Eden' where its environment meets all its needs with the minimum of effort and danger. Nature does not automatically provide food and drink whenever man feels hungry and thirsty. Temperature changes from day-time to night-time. Climate changes from winter to summer and from wet season to dry season. Technology is that element of human culture which man interposes between himself and his physical environment, to exploit that environment more effectively and to protect himself from it. A society will generally select certain elements from its physical environment and through some technological process convert these to a beneficial use. It effects a certain degree of control over its environment and in the process, modifies it and to varying degrees transforms its appearance.

Technology can be defined as the sum total of technical processes known to a society for converting materials found in nature into substances and artifacts required by its culture. Tools are the instruments or the means by which such a conversion is effected. A technique is a way in which raw materials, tools, labor and skill are organized towards reaching a stated goal. To build a canoe, the technological process involves having a set of ideas as to the form and function of the desired canoe, the recruitment and reward of people with the necessary skill to shape and assemble the different pieces that will make up the canoe, the selection of the correct raw materials and the possession of the tools necessary to convert these raw materials into the finished canoe. The canoe in turn is itself a tool. It may be used to transport people or goods from one island to another, or to fish from, or to trade with. Techniques and tools may be used to produce other tools. Primary tools are those used in some direct exploitation of the physical environment. Secondary tools are those used in some technique to produce other tools.

Tools and techniques are not only directed to producing more tools but also to create other objects that do not have a technological function. They may instead have a utilitarian function or denote social status or be used for decorative or symbolic purposes. Tools are therefore a sub-set of a wider category of artifacts that are produced by a technological process from materials found in the natural environment. The sum total of artifacts possessed by members of a society and resulting from some technological process is usually called the material culture of that society. Such a collection of artifacts is assumed to reflect the behavioral activities of the members of a society, and in most cases to be an integral part of them. It is for this reason that ethnographic collections in museums are considered to abstract and display many patterns and themes characteristic of the cultures that they represent. Archaeologists are faced with the problem of reconstructing and explaining past cultures and ways of life from the remnants of the material culture that are recovered from archaeological sites.

Peoples of the world differ widely in the complexity of their material culture and particularly in the efficiency of their technologies. The Australian Aborigines of the central desert, for example, rely on a simple hunting and gathering economy. The men use a throwing stick and a spear and spear-thrower for hunting and a small range of chipped stone implements for cutting, scraping and preparing meat and skins. The women use a digging-stick to grub up roots and tubers and carry bark trays and fiber baskets for the collection of wild grasses and berries. The Australian Aborigines can be compared to the central Eskimo of the Arctic coast of North America whose economy is based on the intensive hunting of animals, fishing and the gathering of wild plants. Their hunting implements include various kinds of spears, the spear-thrower, the harpoon (a spear with a detachable head used particularly in seal and walrus hunting), and the bow and arrow. Smaller animals and birds are caught in traps and snares; fishtraps, fish-spears, nets, hook and line are used to catch salmon trout in the summer. The Eskimo use the light kayak canoe and heavier umiak or open boat for the hunting of seal and walrus and for travel and transport in summer. For traveling over ice and snow in winter they use the dog-sled.

Although both these societies live in harsh, climatically marginal areas of the world, it can be seen that the central Eskimo have elaborated a more specialized technology for the fuller exploitation of the available food resources than have the central desert Aborigines. Similar examples of the presence of a simple technology related to limited food resources and a food-gathering strategy can be seen for the Paiute and Shoshone Indians of the Great Basin of the USA, the pygmies of the Congo basin and the Bushmen of the Kalahari desert. A simple technology may also limit a people to exploiting only a very narrow range of the potential of the environment. With the introduction of the horse by the Spanish in the 16th century the Indians of the great plains of North America were able to specialize in buffalo hunting and extracted most of their food and raw materials from these and other animals. The Indians were then able to move to different areas and to exploit the seasonally available food resources by hunting, fishing and gathering. The agricultural potential of the prairies, however, was first exploited when European colonists settled there and introduced a plow technology and the farming techniques required for this mode of food production.

Human societies present us with a considerable and often bewildering diversity of technological achievements and environmental adaptations. The complexity of apparently simple methods of hunting, of clearing fields for the sowing of crops, the construction of houses and shelters, and the production of the material things needed for everyday life in simple societies is often not realized by urban-dwellers in heavily industrialized societies who are not only surrounded by an artificial, man-made environment but in many ways are oblivious to it. But whatever the complexity of these differing technological systems, there are certain general ends or needs that have to be satisfied in any society. Whatever the variety of particular technologies found in different societies, therefore, they will all bear a relationship to each other in the satisfaction of common, basic human needs. These can be classified here as the need to regulate temperature, the need for sustenance, the need for protection and the need for communication.

First the need to regulate temperatures: man, like other primates, first evolved in the tropical regions of the world and has only managed to inhabit temperate and Arctic regions through technological development. Like other animals, he possesses biological mechanisms such as sweating, respiratory control and the dilation of surface blood-vessels for the internal regulation of body temperature. The different skin colors that people have are caused by varying concentrations of pigment (melanin) in the skin, which protects the underlying tissues and organs from intense solar radiation. However these biological mechanisms have a limited range of adaptation and particularly in the very hot and very cold areas of the world man needs further protection which he himself provides in the form of heat, shelter and clothing.

The discovery of fire to provide heat, light and for cooking was certainly made before the development of our species. We know that homo erectus knew how to use and control fire and probably how to produce it over 300,000 years ago. This first discovery of the harnessing of natural energy is therefore likely to have coincided with the colonization of the sub-tropical and temperate regions of the world by our hominid ancestors. The construction of shelters for protection against rain, cold and intense solar radiation has an antiquity of at least 30,000 years, while human groups have always tended to inhabit natural caves and rock shelters for the same reasons.

Climate is a strong conditioning factor in building shelters and partly accounts for the wide variety in human habitations. The need for insulation from heavy downpours of rain, against extremes of heat and cold – in desert areas of the world, for example, where daytime temperatures of over 100° can drop to freezing point at night – against wind and seasonal changes in climate, and the need for ventilation against high humidity are compelling factors in the structure of shelters (see pages 14-29). Clothing is more directly related to the maintenance of a uniform body temperature, either by insulating the body in cold climates and preventing body heat being dissipated or by facilitating such heat transference in hot climates. The closely tailored skin garments of the Eskimo, for example, are specifically 9 designed to retain body heat, while the long flowing robes of the Beduin Arabs allow maximum circulation of air around the body and the loss of body heat (see pages 58-71). But human shelter and clothing also have a wide range of functions not related to the regulation of body temperature. Clothing in our society, for example, expresses, *inter alia,* gender, age and sexual awareness. Non-utilitarian functions of a similar or different nature are found for the clothing of other peoples as well.

All human societies must have traditional and well-established methods of acquiring the food and drink needed to sustain life. The human body, like any biological organism, is a converter. In other words, it is a biological machine and one of its many functions is to convert food into energy that can be stored and, when used, burnt off by the organism and dissipated as heat.

The techniques of acquiring food in simple societies are generally classified into hunting and gathering economies including specialized hunters like the Eskimo and the Plains Indians; intensive collectors of wild foods like the Bushmen of the Kalahari and the Australian Aborigines and fishermen like the north-west coast Indians of North America. Today only a very small proportion of the peoples of the earth live solely from hunting and gathering but 10,000 years ago it was the only method of acquiring food known to man.

Nomadic pastoralists rely principally on the milk, meat and sometimes blood products from their domesticated animals, which they also trade with settled agricultural peoples for foodstuffs and goods which they cannot produce themselves. In fact pastoralist peoples such as the pastoral Fulani of northern Nigeria or the Masai of Kenya certainly in the present day inhabit geographically marginal areas where agriculture could not be practised and are only able to survive by forming a close, dependent relationship with settled agricultural peoples. Indeed many societies have a mixed pastoral and agricultural economy where men look after the animals, while women and young children or old people are responsible for cultivation.

Agriculture, which includes a wide variety of food-producing economies, has been the most successful economic strategy developed by man, that is until the relatively recent development of industrialized economies. Agriculture formed the economic base to all the old and new world civilizations. It is broadly true that such developments in the complexity of society were possible through the high food yields that only agriculture can produce through the domestication and control of various cereal and root plants. In fact, it is only in the last 100 years that a complex machine technology has been applied to farming and the vast majority of the population in advanced societies has been divorced from satisfying the needs for subsistence farming and is released to find work in expanding urban centers.

The needs of sustenance also require the development of suitable tools and weapons for hunting, collecting, fishing and herding of animals, for clearing vegetation and for sowing, tending and harvesting domesticated plants (see pages 44-57).

The greater part of the food required by a community will be harvested in one period of the year and will have to be preserved and stored to be used over the next economic cycle. Most agricultural societies therefore, particularly those based on the production of cereal foods, have complex methods of storing grain and seeds in their settlements which have to be zealously guarded against thieves and predators. Most foods also have to be prepared before being eaten. This usually involves some method of cooking such as boiling, roasting, steaming or frying. A range of household domestic equipment is therefore needed for cooking and for serving of food and drink, and usually a special area of the house or settlement has to be apportioned for such tasks. A pragmatic distinction exists, therefore, between the activities associated with the procuring of food and those associated with the preparation and serving of food. In many societies it is reflected in a sexual division of labor.

Security of person and of property is a universal need. In many societies this is satisfied by membership of a social group where strong ritual and penal sanctions operate against members who, by offending the rights of another member, offend the group as a whole. In simple societies uncontrolled warfare occurs, therefore, between groups where such sanctions are either very weakly enforced or do not exist at all. Hostilities tend to be intermittent and to be of only short duration since there is no professional group of soldiers, and men will go on raids only when they are not involved in any subsistence activities, or else certain age groups of males will belong to warrior societies (as found among many of the Plains Indian tribes or among many East African pastoralist societies). The warfare that does exist in such societies is as much bound up with motives of vengeance and feuding or the gain of prestige as with the relatively small economic gains which may be won. For example, among the Crow Indians of the Great Plains a man achieved reputation and prestige by the acquisition of war honors. He was rewarded for leading a successful war-party, for capturing an enemy's weapon in combat, for being the first to strike an enemy or for driving off a horse tethered in an enemy camp. The weapons used in such warfare are often an extension of weapons already developed for hunting, together with special additions such as a shield or body-armor for defensive purposes (see pages 100-113).

Protection calls not only for techniques to combat human and animal aggressors but also for means of protecting members of a group from disease, illness and other afflictions which may be considered to be of a supernatural origin. Thus all societies have some means of diagnosing the cause of a particular illness, and have developed a set of techniques for curing such maladies. The symptoms of many diseases place them in a particular folk category for which the treatment is known and immediate. In other cases, particularly where the cause is thought to be of a supernatural origin, some kind of divination will be required to discover the correct cure. The relationship between some kind of supernatural offense and the onset of disease is a fairly general cultural pattern associated with anxieties about various kinds of misfortune. Such curing techniques, and particularly the ceremonial that surrounds the treatment, seem to have two important aspects. Firstly, they allay the anxiety on behalf of the patient, and secondly, they promote social cohesion and support for an afflicted member, since such an event is as much a threat to the well-being of the group as it is to the individual.

No human group lives in isolation, nor can it subsist on the resources immediately available to it. One of the defining characteristics of man is his ability to speak, store and transmit information through social contact and the media of speech and language. One of the features that define human culture is its tradition, the ability for stored information about the ways of doing things to be transmitted from generation to generation.

Speech is the primary method of human communication and, in terms of the complexity of the ideas and information that can be transmitted, it is also the most efficient method. It is the means of communication which we are first aware of. Combined with gestures, facial expressions and general body behavior it becomes an identified aspect of individual personality. Writing is a derivative of speech: an advanced form of writing will have a set of symbols each of which represents a particular spoken sound or phoneme. In the same way, other forms of communication, such as drum-signalling, smoke-signalling, whistling, gesturing, codes and cyphers are all derived from speech. In most cases, such non-verbal forms of communication are devised by man as abbreviated substitutes for speech either to simplify language barriers or to overcome physical distance. A whole range of ethnographic 'musical instruments' therefore have as a primary function the development of a musical language for the transmission of information. Information that will be invaluable for planning activities can also be stored by various devices such as tally-sticks or knotted cords to mark time or the changing of days or seasons, to keep count in some competition or in hunting. It is significant that the first pictographic writing of the Bronze Age Sumerian and Minoan civilizations were economic accounts listing categories of goods received and disposed and the people involved, rather than recording thoughts and ideas.

Art is a major form of non-verbal communication for conveying ideas and information and has certain elements in common with language. In particular, an artistic tradition operates within a defined set of conventions and uses particular media and motifs to create a system of symbols that convey meanings to an audience. The function of art is to reinforce belief, custom and values within a society and art objects are usually produced for a particular, often ritual, context. They also serve to create an atmosphere for the successful transmission of information significant to the culture.

The importance of this cultural need is reflected in the striving for formal excellence and aesthetic appeal. In most cases, the artist operates within a closely limited set of conventions as to what is or is not acceptable to the members of his society who are ultimately the arbiters of cultural ideals. The artist's works are a witness to a wide set of dynamics that operate to identify particular cultures and maintain their cohesion.

Such cohesion depends on opportunity for personal interaction and for ideas and innovations to be exchanged between groups. Thus all societies have means for transporting their members, goods and their more non-tangible cultural possessions in seasonal migrations, trading expeditions, subsistence activities and the visiting of kin and friends in other social groups. The significance of efficient methods of land and water transport can be seen in the relative importance of the exchange of goods and raw materials in different societies; in the aggregates of population that can be maintained by the long distance trade of foodstuffs and other materials; and in specialization of production. An increase in the capacity of transport systems effectively permits a broadening of cultural horizons.

It was through the development of more efficient forms of water transport that European man became aware of the existence of many other cultures besides his own and started to describe the customs and ways of life of these peoples which form one of the beginnings of the modern discipline of anthropology. The boundaries that in the past separated cultures are now rapidly breaking down due to the increasing mobility of the world's population and the development of sophisticated methods of transmitting knowledge, ideas and values from one society to another. In a world where a decision made in a boardroom in London can affect the lives of peoples in Africa, South America or Asia, it is right to emphasize the need for us to learn and share in the variety of human culture through all the methods of communication available to us.

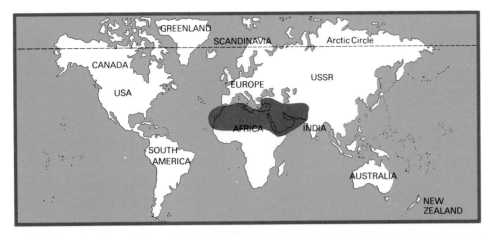

Each chapter in this volume includes a section of photographs and drawings illustrating the artifacts used in each of the eight cultural areas of the world as colored. At the top of each column of illustrations is a map showing their area of origin.

Islamic/Semitic world

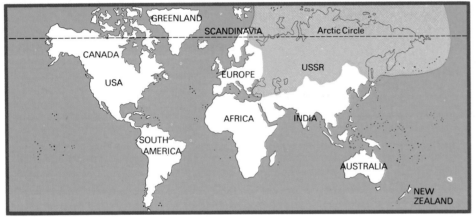

Central and northern Asia

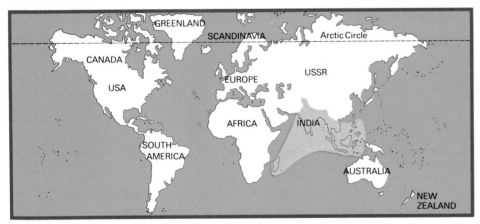

Southern Asia

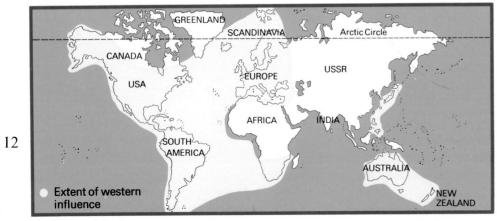

Extent of western influence

Western-dominated world

12

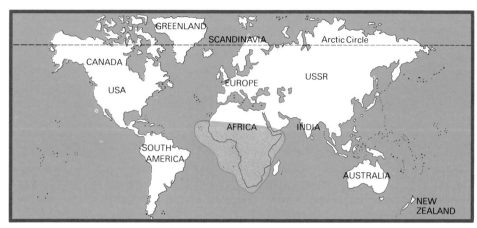

Black Africa

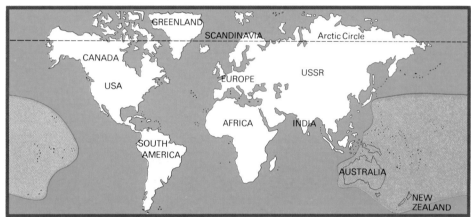

Australasia

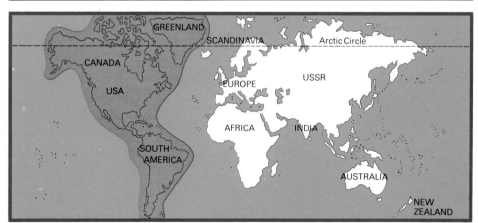

Amerindia

13

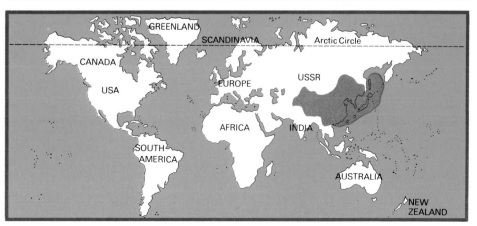

Orient

# Man the builder

15

Function and art
go together because Man
must allow his life meaning . . .
thus Australia's inspired
Sydney Opera House.

In human life, natural environment affects material things more obviously than religious or social ideas, and at a simple level of culture more than at an advanced one. Nowhere is this more clear than in the field of housing. The climate imposes a need for protection from cold, rain, wind or sun. The environment provides the materials. It also imposes a requirement for permanent, temporary or portable dwellings. Even so, man can often exercise a freedom of choice. When the basic demands of the environment have been met, it is cultural factors that become paramount.

Peoples who do not cultivate the soil or depend on livestock, but live by hunting and collecting their food, usually have to live a wandering life. They move round their tribal territories to take advantage of seasonal resources. Such peoples who have survived into modern times include the Australian Aborigines, the Bushmen, the pygmies of the Congo forests, the Hadza of Tanzania and some forest peoples of Malaya. Since they have to move frequently their shelters are temporary. Since they have no means of transport, they normally use materials available at each camp site. The Australians make huts of branches stuck into the ground and covered with leaves, grass or mud, or of sheets of bark. They may make do with a windbreak of branches or bark or banked-up sand, and sleep huddled together with their dogs. Bushmen shelters are equally simple. In the forests the need is for shelter from rain and drip, so side walls may be dispensed with. The large glossy leaves of many forest trees make excellent roofing material.

In America, however, there are some notable exceptions to this general picture of the hunting and collecting life. Many of the Eskimo of northern Canada use the snow house where they spend the winter seal-hunting on the sea ice. The snow house is a most remarkable structure. It is a dome of snow blocks which are laid spirally so that while it is being constructed it is self-supporting. The internal heat from the blubber lamps changes the snow to ice, making it very strong. Windows of clear ice admit light. An inner lining of skins provides insulation. There are descending levels from the living platform to the tunnel entrance which preserve warmth and exclude draughts. In the spring thaw the whole structure disappears without trace. During the summer the Eskimo use caribou skin tents, which they can carry because they have efficient means of land and sea transport: the dog sled and the skin-covered umiak. On the tundra the Caribou Eskimo spend the whole year in skin tents.

The bison hunters of the North American plains followed the migrating herds. In a seasonally harsh climate they needed adequate shelter, and the prairies – except along the river courses – provide no materials. So they developed the teepee. This is a basic framework of three or four poles – tied where they cross at the top, with further poles added all round – covered with bison skins, shaped and sewn together. At the top is an adjustable smoke flap. They were able to carry the teepee with them because, even before they acquired the horse from the white man, they had dog transport. Two poles were crossed on a dog's shoulders the ends trailing on the ground; other dogs carried bundles. Many hunters and reindeer herders of northern Asia use similar tents, covered with skins or bark.

Pastoral nomads who depend on flocks and herds live in those parts of the Old World where scanty rainfall or a short growing season makes agriculture impossible. Most often they are found living in deserts, steppes or tundra, where building materials are lacking. But as they have animals, they have no great difficulty in carrying shelters with them.

The Beduin of the Arabian, Jordanian and Syrian deserts use tents of goat-hair cloth obtained from the settled Arabs of the desert borders. These 'black tents', which may be quite elaborate, consist basically of a strip supported on ropes between pairs of poles, with a back and a front curtain. Many peoples of western Asia and north Africa use similar tents. The tents of the Kazakh and other horse and sheep herders of the Turkistan steppes are quite different in design. They have a circular wall which is a collapsible trellis of willow rods pierced and tied with hide thongs where they cross. On top of this further rods curve inwards to a wood ring, which forms a smoke hole. The whole structure is covered with sheets of felt, made from the wool of their sheep, and is furnished with camel-hair rugs. Willow grows in the river valleys. The tent can be quickly dismantled or erected and is carried by a bactrian camel. The use of this type of tent extends across the Siberian steppe and into Iran and Anatolia. The harsh climate compels the Kazakh to spend the winter in the semi-subterranean houses with stone or sod walls, roofed with poles and turf, built in groups in the river valleys.

The Lapp reindeer herders of central and north Norway and Sweden have yet another type of tent. It looks like a squat teepee superficially, but it has a more complex wooden frame. Parts of the frame peg together. Against these, poles are leaned all round. Traditionally this kind of tent was covered with skins in winter and birch-bark in summer. More recently it has been covered instead with horse-blankets and canvas. Reindeer either drawing sledges or as pack animals provide the transport for these tents. Like the Kazakh, the Lapps had winter settlements. These were in the 'church villages', where the children could go to school. Nowadays only the young men follow the herds.

Permanent houses go with a settled life. For most of humanity this has followed the adoption of agriculture as the basic means of subsistence. The development of urban life and specialists – craftsmen, priests, soldiers, administrators – depended on an agricultural population producing more food than they needed for themselves.

Although highly-organized communities may import materials for important buildings, they tend to be weighty and bulky and this has ensured that until modern times the main reliance for materials must be on local sources.

In the greater part of the world wood is the most plentiful and appropriate material for building houses. It is easily worked, even with stone tools. It is relatively easy to transport by land or water. It often grows into convenient shapes and sizes. And it is strong and flexible. In the majority of houses that are made mainly of other materials it is used, for instance, for roofing or flooring. Its main disadvantages are its inflammability and its susceptibility to attack by insects.

A very ancient form of house in the Old World, especially in the pine belts of northern Asia, Europe and the Himalayas, is the log house. This requires quantities of straight logs, which are laid horizontally and cut away where they cross so that they fit closely together to form a box, usually but not necessarily four-sided. The chinks between the logs are plugged with moss, mud or turf. The structure rests on the surface, requires no substantial foundation, and may when it is removed or finally collapses leave little archaeological evidence except its hearth. It was taken to the new world and widely adopted by colonists in North America. Greek architecture has many features which show its derivation from the log hut and other simple wood forms of houses.

The log house is expensive in its use of timber. In places where soft woods are not plentiful, or where climatic conditions are not so difficult and a less substantial construction is acceptable, the timber framed house takes its place. In the tropical forests of South America, in Africa and Asia as well as in the Pacific islands and the temperate zones the timber framed house is found in varying forms. Its basic structure is a rectangular, square or sometimes circular frame which supports the roof. The walls are of skin and are often added last. The ridge pole is usually supported by two or more center posts. Rafters run from the ridge-pole to the wall plates, which are borne by posts at the corners and usually at points along the walls. The rafters support purlins – horizontal members which carry the roofing material. The structure may be much more complex, but the distinctive feature of this type of house is that the walling material does not support the roof.

Timber houses of this kind are sometimes very large and architecturally impressive. The men's houses of the Purari delta in Papua were as much as 24 meters high at the front gable. The ancestor cult houses of the Abelam, in northern New Guinea, are 15 meters high and decorated to the peak with complex paintings of ancestral spirits. These houses are usually constructed by lashing the parts together with vines or cordage. Iron nails are either not available or too expensive, and drilling holes for pegging is difficult, especially with stone tools.

The 'half-timbered' houses of Britain and Europe depended on a developed carpentry technique, as the parts were mortised and pegged, and on efficient iron tools. The simplest form of 'half-timbered' house, still to be seen in English villages, is made by the cruck method. The ridge pole is borne at each end by a pair of substantial curved members, sometimes made by splitting a single suitably-shaped branch. These also support cross members at the height of the eaves. To these cross members wall plates are attached. In this way the walls can be vertical and the interior as spacious as possible. The walls of these houses were usually made of wattle and daub. When wattle and daub was replaced by brick filling this was nevertheless not load-bearing. As carpentry techniques improved half-timbered houses attained the complexity of such famous examples as those of the west midlands of England or the Rhineland towns.

In England and other parts of Europe timber was replaced as a building material by stone or brick as the forests were depleted. Outside Europe fired brick is unusual as a traditional material although sun-dried mud bricks are widely used in favorable conditions.

In the grass plains of Africa timber is scarce and the houses are adapted accordingly. 'Beehive' huts are hemispherical and consist of a framework of flexible 17 poles pushed into the ground in a circle, bent down and tied where they overlap, and covered with grass thatch. Similar huts are made on the plains of northern Asia. The other characteristic type of hut of savanna Africa is made by sticking poles in the ground in a circle to form vertical walls, which are covered with mud plaster or thatch. A conical roof, often made separately on the ground, is fitted on to this and thatched. The thatch is sometimes laid to form distinct layers described as the Nilotic flounce. These huts rarely have center posts. The roof is a single unit supported by the walls.

Stone is relatively uncommon as a house-building material among modern peasants and tribal peoples outside Europe. It is generally used in arid areas where other materials are scarce, or in mountainous regions where warmth and substantial construction are necessary. Dry-stone buildings are common in the highland zone from Iran to western China and in parts of South America. These houses sometimes have two storeys, although the upper storey may be of timber. The end walls are often raised to form gables which support the ridge pole. The roof structure is nearly always of timber.

Knowledge of the true arch and of the vault is almost entirely restricted to the areas of ancient civilization, which explains why timber is so generally used for roofing. An alternative method of roofing in stone, which is well known in the ancient world (including America) and can still be found in places down the east side of Africa, is corbelling. By this technique horizontal layers of stone are progressively overlapped inwards until the remaining gap can be closed with a single large stone. The space which can be covered by this method is limited. And unless the walls are massive the structure is unstable. African corbelled huts are therefore small and usually circular or oval. This roofing method has survived until today in the Mediterranean area.

Mud is only appropriate as a structural material in relatively hot and arid climates. Mud will stand quite heavy rain if it is dried out by hot sun afterwards, provided water cannot penetrate inside the walls and if the foundations are dry. But it collapses in prolonged damp conditions. So mud walls are sometimes built on stone foundations, and the houses often have wide low eaves. Mud in the form of pisé (rammed earth) has been used as a material in some parts of England. Mud as a plaster, sometimes mixed with a binding material such as cow hair, has been used from northern Europe to the tropics.

When mud is the main building material it is generally used in one of two ways. Although the technique of building with sun-dried mud bricks is similar to that of building in stone or fired brick, the load-bearing capacity of mud brick is less and the walls consequently have to be thicker and often have a marked batter. The technique is very important to the archaeologists and is still widely practised in the drier parts of the Afro-Asian area and in America where it is called by the Spanish name, adobe.

By the other method of building with mud, plastic mud is modeled by hand. Successive layers are added as the ones below dry. Some tribes of northern Nigeria build two-storied domed houses by this method; the upper floor is supported by a modeled mud arch, and internal fittings – storage bins, beds, benches – are modeled during building. The dome is thatched to protect it from rain.

Reeds are not widely used as a main building material. Probably the best example from the modern world of this kind of building comes from the Madan, the marsh Arabs of Iraq. The reeds, which grow to a height of twenty feet or more, are bound in large bundles. These are either set in the ground upright, as if they were large posts, or curved over to form a series of arches. Strong reed matting forms the outer cover. Large and impressive guest-halls are built by these methods. Reeds have a wider importance as a subsidiary material for thatching, making mats for things like wall covers and screens.

Building houses on piles, or stilts, to raise the floor above ground level has many advantages. In mountainous districts it means that houses can be built on rough or sloping ground. In hot climates it allows the air to circulate. It provides some protection against human enemies and against dangerous animals. And it provides space underneath for storage or livestock. Over water it makes it easy to move by boat and easy to dispose of refuse. It gives safety from floods and may be the only means by which riverine or delta areas, with rich resources in fish or sago (as in New Guinea), can be inhabited. Pile building has been practised from prehistoric Europe to present-day Melanesia. Many peoples in apparently identical situations, however, build on the ground.

If the demands of the environment and the resources it offers regulate the form of dwellings to some degree there remains a wide area in which human choice can operate. The individual can exercise choice on minor matters such as decorative details. But choice is to a far greater degree governed by cultural attitudes. Some types of religion or of social organization, for example, require temples, cult centers or places of assembly to be built. The great Maya centers of central America, the Polynesian sacred sites – which took the form of paved and walled courts of massive stepped platforms – are examples of this kind of building from peoples whose domestic architecture was simple and ephemeral.

The influence of social factors is especially clearly seen in the way buildings are allocated to people. Europeans and North Americans usually regard the family – of parents and children with perhaps an aged grandparent or a son- or daughter-in-law – as the normal unit for housing. So do many other peoples throughout the world. But there are also many peoples who do not. Some tribes of the Amazon basin, New Guinea, Borneo and Burma, for example, have large houses which shelter a whole community. In these longhouses each family usually has its own area and its own hearth, perhaps partitioned off. The longhouses in Borneo differ in being in effect a row of individual family dwellings, each built side by side on piles but under one continuous roof, with an internal thoroughfare running the whole length.

Some peoples have houses in which bachelors, or all the men, live and sleep together. In parts of the highlands of New Guinea there is a feeling that close contact with women is dangerous to the masculinity on which success in life depends. Among these peoples each family has its own house which the men frequent by day. But at night all males except the very young and the very old retire to the men's house. The men's house is frequently the place where sacred objects are kept, ceremonies are prepared, and community affairs are discussed. The men's house has, in most of its forms, two functions: it provides a means of keeping ritual matters or community affairs from women – who however have other ways of exerting influence – and it ensures that the men are assembled, with their weapons handy, in case of surprise attack.

The compound system, common in west Africa, helps to resolve some of the problems arising from polygamy. The family compound is surrounded by a wall. This usually has a single entrance which may open into a sort of guardroom. Inside the compound each wife has her own quarters: a room or a separate hut. There will also be store-rooms and other domestic offices. Among Muslim peoples the female section is not accessible to male visitors, who do not penetrate beyond the forecourt.

Social factors also govern a people's general settlement pattern and the planning of their villages. Where warfare is frequent, defense considerations may be the decisive factor in how the villages are sited. In the New Guinea mountains hamlets are often sited on steep-sided spurs. The coastal Solomon Islanders set their villages back from the shore behind a screen of trees, where they will be invisible to raiders from the sea. The Amazon tribes build their communal houses near but out of sight of rivers for the same reason. Villages are protected by stockades, and towns by walls, in many parts of the world. The Maori of New Zealand not only built substantial palisades round their villages, which were sited in naturally strong positions, but surrounded them with earthworks comparable to those of the iron age Celts. Some people built watch-towers. Houses built in trees have been recorded quite widely, though they are usually refuges in time of war, or from wild animals, rather than permanent dwellings.

The restrictions of a defensive site may largely determine how houses are placed in villages and towns. Where they do not some peoples divide the settlement into wards, each occupied by a clan or some other social sub-division, or – in more sophisticated urban societies – by a trade. Other settlements have rigidly-prescribed plans: a street is closed at one end by the chief's house or the men's house, or houses are set round a dancing ground. Sometimes house sites belong to clans, and are left vacant if no member of the clan wishes to use them. Many peoples live very much in public. Others, such as the people who live in compounds in west Africa, have a high degree of privacy, but meet at the mosque, the council house or the market place.

Some peoples do not have villages or hamlets at all. Many Polynesian tribespeople's houses were scattered individually about their valleys. Some New Guinea highlanders, who also live in scattered single houses, say that it is safer to live like this. A hamlet can be surprised, they say, but in an open valley an attack on one house warns the others.

Dwellings, temples, meeting houses and defense works are by no means the only structures made by peoples at a tribal level. Pens may be needed for domestic animals. People who grow grain need food stores, for cereals must be reaped when they are ripe, whereas most tropical root crops (yams are an exception) can be left in the ground for a time but do not keep after lifting. Bridges range from one tree felled across a mountain torrent to large and elaborate suspension bridges of rattan or liana with built-up abutments. There are also people, especially in the far east, who live permanently on boats.

19

In Australia's outback an Aboriginal woman carries a load of spinifex bushes to roof her shelter.

(Over page) An aerial view of a village in the Ethiopian highlands shows the concentric arrangement of family dwellings within protective fences.

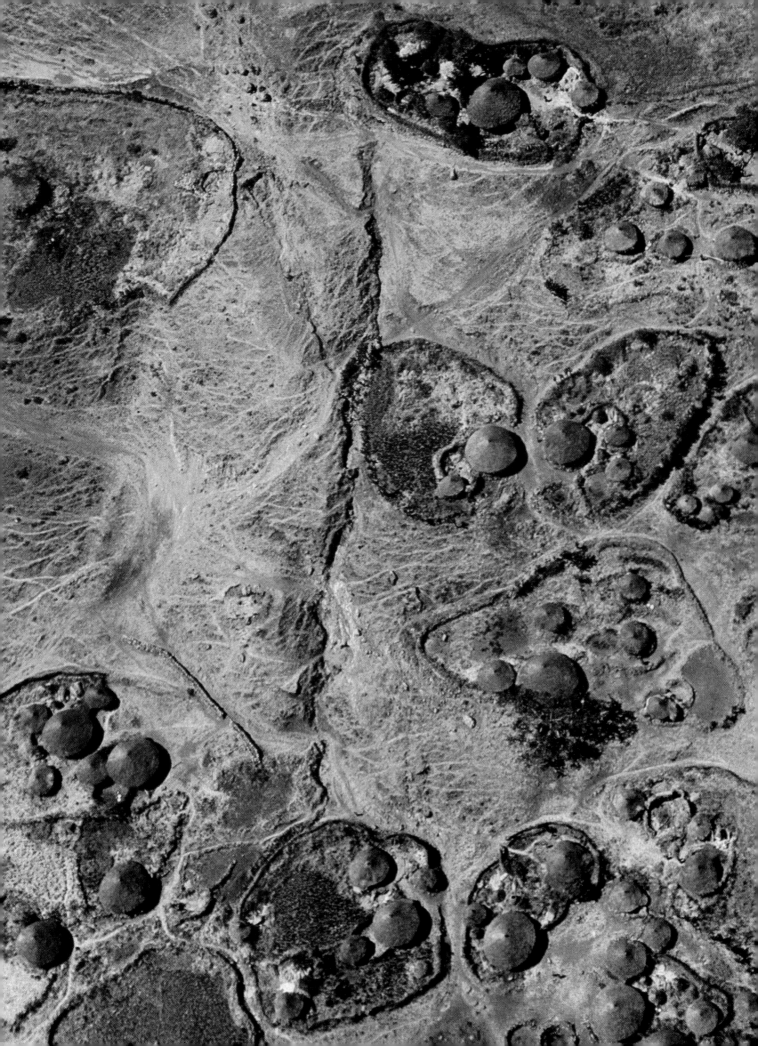

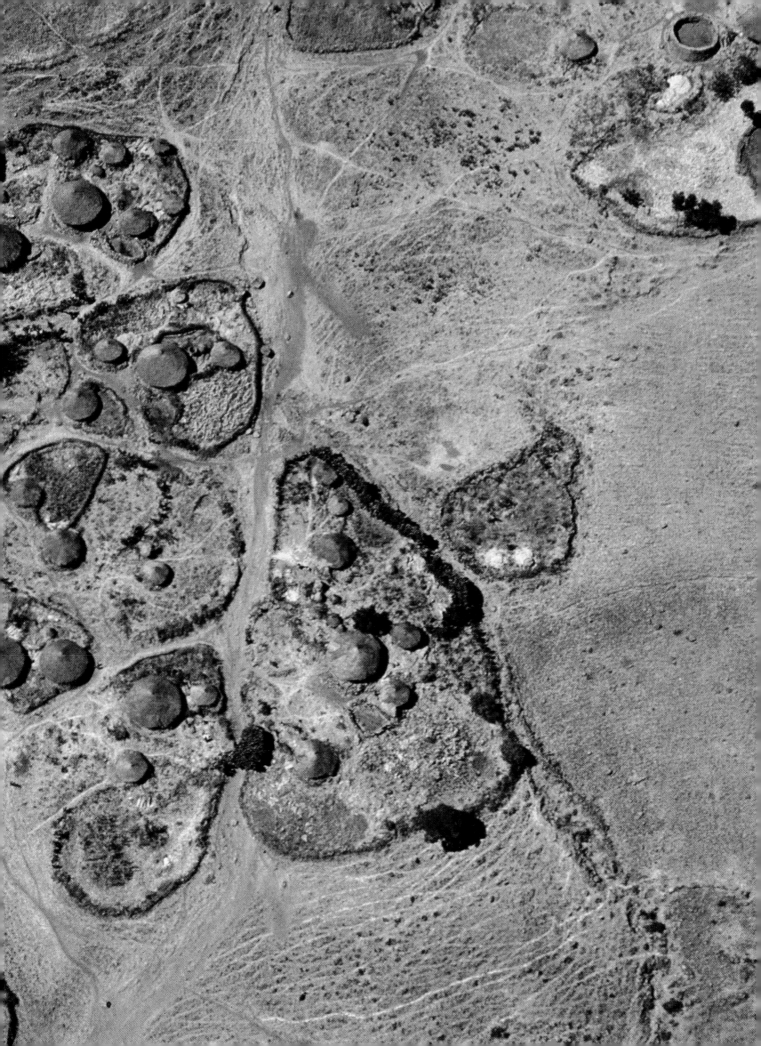

# Man the builder

A grain store in Mali, west Africa, shows the mud structure braced with tamarisk logs so widespread in the region.

Ladakh, on the Tibet-Kashmir border is famous for its monasteries and rock carvings. It is one of the earliest centers of Lamaist Buddhism, and many of these carvings date from the 10th century.

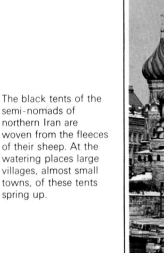

St Basil's Cathedral, Moscow was built in the 16th century and still dominates Red Square with its striped onion domes. Originall[y] built to celebrate the Russian victory over the Tatars, it is now a museum piece.

The black tents of the semi-nomads of northern Iran are woven from the fleeces of their sheep. At the watering places large villages, almost small towns, of these tents spring up.

The mud-built house with domed roof is common throughout the Muslim countries of the middle east, but these examples show a further refinement — periscope-shaped ventilators in the roof.

The inhabitants of Kamchatka, Siberia, build a dual-purpose dwelling with winter and summer quarters. The illustration shows a drawing of one made on Captain Cook's third voyage. I[n] the foreground is the semi-underground winter house, which is entered through a hole in the conical roof. In the background are th[e] summer huts on stilts. The two types of dwelling would normally occupy different sites.

## Southern Asia

The Maharana of Udaipur stands on the steps of his ancestral palace, a 16th century building overlooking the man-made Lake Pichola. Situated in the hills of Rajasthan, the huge palace is now a museum.

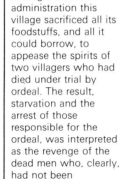

A longhouse in South Vietnam. During the French administration this village sacrificed all its foodstuffs, and all it could borrow, to appease the spirits of two villagers who had died under trial by ordeal. The result, starvation and the arrest of those responsible for the ordeal, was interpreted as the revenge of the dead men who, clearly, had not been successfully appeased.

This temple at Bangli in Bali, with its many-tiered structure, reflects the influence of the Chinese pagoda and the elaborate temples of Burma.

## Western-dominated world

Little Moreton Hall in Cheshire, England, is possibly the finest example of a moated manor house extant. Greater peace and prosperity during the 15th and 16th centuries meant more comfortable and weatherproof houses could be built. But the need for some protection persisted into the late 16th century, especially in border areas like Cheshire. In addition, Moreton Hall is an almost flamboyant example of the timbered style of building. A framework of criss-crossed timbers supports walls of wattle and daub, or, in more advanced cases, brick.

The Black house was the home of Scottish crofters in the western highlands until well into this century. Walls of roughly hewn stone were built without mortar. The floor was of beaten earth, and the roof of thatch, often weighed down with stones against Atlantic gales. Often the corners of the house were rounded, to reduce wind noise during winter storms. A similar form of building can still be seen in the west of Ireland.

Salisbury cathedral, England, is a fine example of the many perpendicular buildings erected to the glory of God throughout Christendom during the 13th and 14th centuries. The term perpendicular derives from the tall gothic arches used in the interior of these cathedrals that give the impression of soaring height.

23

# Man the builder

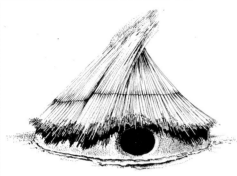

A reed thatched mud hut from sub-Saharan Africa shows several features common to dwellings in swampy areas. The high-pitched roof, essential where rainfall is heavy, rests on a low circular mud wall. A channel round the base of the house diverts water (acting on the same principle as a damp course). The circular entrance keeps out snakes and rats.

The *whare whakairo*, or meeting house, remains the center of village life for the Maori of New Zealand. Still built with the ornate symbolic carvings that have decorated them for centuries, they have served to keep alive Maori tradition and culture.

Built on a raised platform of earth, this huge Fijian grass-mat house is both cool and dry. The steeply pitched roof and grass walls indicate very sophisticated thatching techniques, and the cone-shaped 'porch' over each door bears this out. The thatch is stitched into the palm fronds wrapped round the ridgepole.

The Dogon of Mali and Volta build mud-walled compounds with thatched-roof dwellings and store-houses. The villages are sited close to a cliff on a steep hillside to leave better, more manageable land free for cultivation. The mud and thatch make an ideal building combination for the arid region where the Dogon live, giving cool shady interiors.

The eaves of this house in New Guinea are painted red and white. These ceremonial 'lean-to' houses are built by the Abelam of north-eastern New Guinea. Famed for their elaborate decorative arts, they paint the back of these houses with the faces of the clan spirits.

Reminiscent of the beehive huts of the Celtic monks, this stone-built hut is, in fact, from central Africa. One of the most ancient building techniques where roofing materials are scarce, 'corbelling' consists of using the strength of a circular building to support the gradual inward inclination of the walls, eventually forming a complete cone-shaped structure.

Amerindia

Flat roofs, small windows, these adobe (mud) houses of the Taos Indians in New Mexico show features common to hot climate houses all over the world.

Known to every schoolboy, the wigwam, or teepee, of the North American Plains Indians. The tent material is of buffalo hide decorated with emblems and paintings of beasts of the chase. A flap opens at the top to allow smoke to escape. Like the dwellings of all nomads, the teepee is easily dismantled and moved.

This curiously shaped building is the ceremonial house of the Kogi Indians of northern Colombia. Built of grass, it has at its apex a shelf containing broken pottery and other ceremonial objects. In front stands a line of ceremonial seats, shaped from the local granite.

Orient

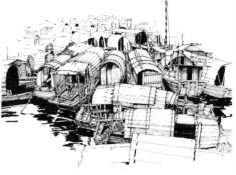

Hong Kong's city on the water. Over-crowding compels a large part of Hong Kong's population to live in junks and houseboats. Roofed with bamboo matting each of these small boats may house a family, or more.

This Taoist temple near Taipai, Taiwan, is a modern reconstruction in the traditional style. The forest on the hill behind has been landscaped to suit the temple. The bottom half of the building is reinforced concrete, and the ornamentation is painted and gilded ceramic. There is a small Taoist monastery nearby.

One of the finest multi-storey pagodas in China. Originally introduced from India, the pagoda has become identified with China, and with Chinese Buddhism in particular.

25

# Man the builder

In addition to the tents made of the hides of their camels, the Tuareg also use huts put together from straw mats. Easy to dismantle and transport. these huts are also comfortable and cool.

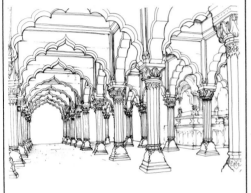

Built between 1639 and 1648 the ruling Moguls of India built the Divan-I-Am in Delhi. It was used for the Emperor to hold public audiences. It represents the height of the great flowering of Muslim building in India in the 17th century.

The Marsh Arabs of Iraq have adapted ingeniously to their unique environment. Probably no other people in the world live so exclusively on the products of marshland. Here a typical Marsh Arab house is illustrated. The reed predominates as a building material, the walls being made of upright reeds bound together by transverse bundles of reeds, while the roof is composed of straw mats, also woven from reeds. Alas, plans to drain the marshlands of the Tigris and Euphrates delta, may bring the Marsh Arab's way of life to an end.

This Lapp tent from Arctic Asia shows many similarities with the North American Indian *teepee*. The same conical structure of poles is used to support a covering of skins or woven cloth, and the same gap is used for smoke to escape. Often a low wall of stones is built as a base for the tent.

The importance of Ladakh as a center of Lamaist Buddhism has already been noted. Here a typical Lamaist monastery tops a small hill in a Ladakh valley. The slab sides of the hilltop building are typical of Tibetan architecture, and may also be seen in the Dalai Lama's palace at Lhasa.

The *yurt* from Siberia is another variant of the skin-covered wood frame tent. Longer and more spacious than the tent of the Lapps or the North American *teepee*, the yurt is in use mainly among the nomadic tribes of Mongolia.

26

## Southern Asia

Cool, lightly built and airy, this Malayan house follows a pattern common all over the far east. Raised on stilts as a protection against vermin as well as flood, the walls are made of bamboo matting. The roof is also made of bamboo, but can also be made of *attap*, the leaves of a palm tree cut down the middle and laid over each other with the leaves pointing in different directions. Both are almost completely waterproof, as, indeed, they need to be in the heavy monsoon rains.

The Bajau of the Philippines live not only in houses built over the sea on stilts, but also in boats. Their building materials are dominated by the palm tree. Its fibers, leaves and wood are used freely both in their houses and boats.

The concave roof with pointed, overhanging eaves is found throughout the Indonesian islands, but most typically in Sumatra. The pointed overhang allows light into the building, but excludes direct sunlight.

## Western-dominated world

Built for the 1967 Montreal Expo, this complex of dwellings, simply called Habitat, represents the dilemma in which modern architects find themselves. Faced with demands for more housing and ever-rising costs of material and space, the units designed for living get smaller and smaller, and cheaper and cheaper. No amount of interesting juggling with angles and shapes can conceal that what the architect is offering here is a series of boxes.

The Pirelli building in Milan is another example of the colossal, dehumanizing scale of much modern commercial and industrial architecture that now dominates so many western cities. Too late, after the damage has been done, are architects beginning to realize that their belief in perfect function creating perfect beauty has been misplaced.

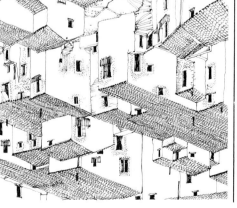

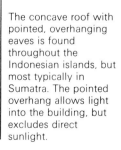

In sharp contrast to the Pirelli building are these whitewashed, ridge-tiled houses in Sicily. The 'rabbit warren' effect striven after by the architect of 'Habitat' (above) has here been achieved by years of haphazard building in a local style with local materials.

# Man the builder

## Black Africa

The Nanzoa of Rhodesia build a storage hut on stilts as a protection against rats and snakes.

The nomads of the Aïr Mountains, Niger, build these dome-shaped huts of grass on a wooden frame. Shown are the frame and a completed hut.

This beehive-shaped grass hut from South Africa took only three days to build. The interior would be very formal, decorated with colored mats and rugs.

## Australasia

Australian Aborigines sit outside their grass hut, Grass is heaped on a wood frame; the thicker the heap of grass, the cooler the interior of the hut.

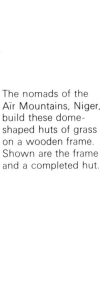

In the islands of Melanesia some tribes pursue the custom of placing virgins in isolation when a marriage is being arranged. They are placed in a tree hut similar to this one, while the unmarried men keep a vigil at the foot of the ladder.

The Jalé of the New Guinea Highlands build settlements of anything between two dozen and 100 huts. Each hut has a wall of wooden planks. Four central poles support conical roof made from leaves or bark. The huts are built in family groups, clustering round the man of the family's hut, invariably the largest one.

28

## Amerindia

The igloo of the Eskimo is made of perhaps the most unlikely building material of all — ice. Built in blocks cut to shape beforehand, once well frozen together, the igloo is virtually indestructible. The small tunnel entrance is more to exclude cold than polar bears.

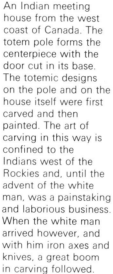

An Indian meeting house from the west coast of Canada. The totem pole forms the centerpiece with the door cut in its base. The totemic designs on the pole and on the house itself were first carved and then painted. The art of carving in this way is confined to the Indians west of the Rockies and, until the advent of the white man, was a painstaking and laborious business. When the white man arrived however, and with him iron axes and knives, a great boom in carving followed.

The Aymara of Lake Titicaca, Peru live in totora reed houses built on floating platforms of reed. Their boats, too, are made of reeds — tapered bundles lashed together to form canoe-like platforms.

## Orient

Like other oriental peoples the Japanese have relied heavily on bamboo in their building techniques. This Gassho-style farmhouse in the Toyama prefecture, has wood and bamboo walls and framework and a roof of dense grass thatch ridged with bamboo slats.

The Summer Palace in Peking, China, once represented the peak of Chinese cultural life. In addition to the merits of the building itself, it contained treasures (pottery, fabrics, painting, sculpture) literally beyond price from all of China's dynasties. Unfortunately the Summer Palace was looted by British troops in the 19th century, and many of the treasures were stolen and scattered. The building itself remains a museum.

# Man the home-maker

Furniture, which is perhaps of central significance in the western housewife's conception of 'home', is nevertheless only one kind of material object involved in everyday domestic life. We chairbound westerners might find it difficult to put ourselves literally in the position of those peoples in the world, such as the village Hindu, who do not sit upon chairs but squat on their haunches when working or relaxing. A Kalahari Bushman lying in bed upon an interior sprung mattress would find himself worlds away from the customary animal hide spread on the ground. He might find himself equally far away from the netted string hammock of the South American Indian or the elaborately carved wooden head-rest of the Papuan. The way people sit or lie is culturally influenced; people of oriental cultures would find an occidental chair highly uncomfortable, while many Europeans would have problems sitting for long periods cross-legged on a mat. On the other hand, the Nigerian Ibibio's stout chairs, benches and beds made out of pieces of raffia-palm midrib slotted and pegged together, would fetch high prices in Heal's furniture shop in London; and the Nigerian Tiv's low bed carved from a solid log was found most comfortable by the author!

Among the nomadic buffalo hunters of the American Great Plains, in the well-furnished Cheyenne lodge, each person had a *chaise longue* and bed. This was constructed from an earth bench padded with grass, and equipped with back-rests covered with buffalo robes which also served as cupboards for storage of foods and other goods. Even among nomadic groups such as the Cheyenne, whose household furniture is greatly restricted because their homes are mobile structures, there is a tendency for people to surround themselves with beautiful objects on which to sit or lie. A simple domestic object such as a wooden stool, in a region such as west Africa, becomes an article of great craftsmanship and artistic expression, borne on the head of a servant following the village chief to a public meeting, or sat upon by a wife pounding yams for dinner in the back yard of her compound. Among the Ashanti of Ghana the royal stool is elevated to the status of an object of veneration intimately connected with the spiritual well-being of the tribe. A deposed Ashanti chief is described as having been 'de-stooled'.

In fact the possession of tools with which to cut and scrape is a more basic need than that of furniture. Stone tools are the earliest known artifacts, and Stone Age cultures have survived until the present day. Siliceous rocks such as flint, chert, and obsidian, chipped to make either flake or core-tools, provide highly effective cutting edges. Some Australian Aborigines were renowned for their advanced methods of chipping flint, and later bottle glass, to produce a wide variety of implements. Stone tools are generally hafted. In this craft the Eskimo excel with their carved knife and scraper handles of

walrus ivory, horn, or wood, tailor-made for the hand. The Admiralty Islanders of Melanesia skilfully fashion knives from long flakes of black obsidian which are hafted in resin handles decorated with geometric patterns. Stone or wooden pestles and mortars, and stone querns for the mashing, pounding and grinding of foodstuffs are in active use throughout most of the world.

Some folk do not have access to ample resources of stone with which to make domestic implements. So they use other materials. Cutting edges are provided by mollusc shells, which can be subjected to many different techniques of manufacture, such as chipping, grinding and perforating. The inhabitants of the coral atolls of the Pacific have relied heavily upon the shell of the giant clam in this respect. Antler and bone are among other materials used to make domestic implements. Some Plains Indians, for example, employed buffalo rib bones for cutting soft substances. In many parts of the world spoons and ladles are carved from wood, or made from shell or horn. Horn can be softened and shaped after soaking in water and heating. An ingenious device is the bamboo knife of Oceania, the blade of which can be 'sharpened' as required by stripping away fresh sections of wood from the cutting edge.

Metal has great advantages of strength and durability for manufacturing many kinds of material objects,

A man of the Chitral valley in Pakistan mixes ground hemp with water to make hashish. The jug, too, is the work of the villagers' hands.

although it is not, unless imported from the outside world, generally a prominent material in the range of domestic objects of pre-industrial peoples. The modern availability of scrap metal has resulted in the decline of primitive iron smelting in Africa. Of great utility, however, are the abundant knives and other tools forged by African smiths from pieces of old oil drums or discarded vehicle springs and then mounted in wooden handles.

In western culture, the hearth is an important symbol of domesticity. People of all cultures use fire for cooking and lighting, and for warming and drying, particularly in colder and damp climates. Making and using fire are thus basic techniques to virtually all mankind, although the Andaman Islanders are frequently cited as having no traditional method of fire-making. The two main methods of making fire are by friction and by percussion. Friction methods involve the use of wood, and include the process of *sawing*, in which one stick is rubbed across the grain of another, *plowing*, in which one stick is rubbed with the grain of another, and *drilling*, in which a cylinder of wood is rotated in another stationary piece of wood. Fire-making by percussion involves striking a spark either from flint with steel or pyrites, or from pyrites with pyrites. The Burmese and a few other peoples use a sophisticated device called a fire-piston, which generates heat by the compression of air in a cylinder.

All peoples use containers of some kind to transport, prepare, and store food and other essential materials of life. Some containers require very little manufacture before use. Mollusc shells, for example, are sometimes employed for carrying water and boiling food. In the Andamans various types of mollusc shell are used as drinking vessels and food receptacles. Tortoise shells may be used as receptacles, and many people in different parts of the world cook tortoises in their shells. The Bushmen use ostrich eggs for water carrying and storage. Unprepared animal tissue can also be used in various ways. Some Amerindian groups, for example, use a paunch for cooking by way of a pot-boiler. Breadfruit can be cooked in its skin, and meat in a melon with its top cut off. In South-east Asia, Melanesia and South America bamboo stems are used for storing and cooking both liquids and solids. When they are used for cooking, sap in the green tissues of the stems reduces inflammability so that the contents are cooked before the stems burn through. Gourds and calabash vessels are even more widely used, commonly for storing liquids and solids and as serving receptacles. Gourds and calabashes may be 'trained' to grow into the required shapes. In many areas they are given complex decorative designs by techniques such as carving, staining and scorching.

Wooden vessels are particularly important in some areas. Simple vessels may be fashioned from bark, the best known example being the birchbark containers of the northern forests. The Shom Pen tribe of Great Nicobar Island make a cooking vessel of bark folded and secured by posts stuck in the ground. A fire is lit below it. Evaporation of water from the utensil's walls reduces its temperature so that it does not burn, in the same way that a cardboard box full of water can be made to boil on a layer of glowing embers. It is in Oceania and on the north-west coast of America, however, that the use of wooden vessels is most highly developed. Carved wooden vessels are used for boiling food by dropping red-hot stones into the contents. In parts of Oceania food is displayed and served at feasts from gigantic wooden troughs and bowls. In Polynesia wooden bowls are prominent in the ceremonial drinking of *kava*. The north-west coast Indians produced a wide range of containers made from wood, including buckets, kettles, urinals and storage chests. Small vessels were carved from a block of wood, while larger containers were carpentered. In both regions, wooden containers were often decorated with highly conventionalized carvings.

There are in some instances containers made of stone. The Australian Aborigines used natural or artificially deepened rock pits for storing water and cooking with heated stones. In Upper Egypt and in many parts of North America people use pots carved from steatite (or soapstone) for cooking. Large and small stone cooking pots are made by hand or on a special lathe in Persia, and in Tibet stone cooking vessels are hollowed from the lump of stone by hand with a special hooked iron implement.

Basketry is of two types, plaited and coiled, and both occur in great variety. There are many different techniques of basket manufacture involving a wide range of materials – usually plant fibers and derived from stems, roots, bark or leaves – which can easily be found in most environments. Baskets are frequently used to gather and store foodstuffs and as all-purpose receptacles. Some forms of baskets are more specialized, such as the clay-lined basketry trays in which seeds, crickets and meat were roasted by the Coconinos of Arizona. The Californian Indians are regarded as having reached the epitome of technical and artistic excellence in basketry and produced baskets so tightly woven that they were water-tight. These were used for boiling food on hot stones. Baskets can also be made water-tight by being coated with an impervious layer such as pitch.

Many of the containers described above illustrate that certain of the qualities which are often ascribed entirely to pottery are in fact also possessed by other types of vessel. For example, bamboo-stem cooking survives among groups who must travel light, and prefer the taste of rice cooked in bamboo. Simple vessels such as shells, calabashes, bamboo and coconut shells are readily available in the places where they are used and require minimum processing. Stone pots are often stronger and more durable than pottery ones. Baskets are light-weight and strong. The relative efficiency of certain non-ceramic containers may help to explain why some folk prefer not 31 to make or use pottery. Nevertheless possession of pot-making skills has been taken to indicate that a certain stage has been attained in cultural development.

Pots and potting are not exclusively associated with the sedentary agricultural life. The Bushmen of some parts of the Kalahari made their own pottery and this was decorated with characteristic impressed motifs. The Andamanese who are also nomadic hunters and gatherers produce highly serviceable and well-made pots. The cattle-herding Hottentots produce surprisingly large pots of over three gallons' capacity. Many pastoralists use pottery although they may not themselves make it, as they are inclined to disdain craftwork – for example the Arab pastoral groups who obtain pots from the *fellahin* (Egyptian peasants) and the Kenyan Boran who get theirs from despised Konso craftsmen called *hauda*. There are groups of peripatetic potters in all continents except Australia. Adaptations of pottery vessels for easy carriage among both settled and nomadic peoples show that pots are not necessarily the non-mobile fragile articles that they are commonly supposed to be. Hottentot pots are specially designed to be transported by ox. They are oval in section and have lugs to which can be attached cords to hang them by. Special carrying devices for water-pots are employed by such widely separated peoples as the Monpa of the north-west frontier of India and the inhabitants of the American south-west who have a range of special pottery 'canteens'.

It is frequently assumed that, as pots belong naturally to the context of the domestic hearth, potting in pre-industrial society is exclusively the realm of women. Pottery production for the home is generally female work, but there are many contradictory examples, especially from south-west Africa where among many groups primitive potting is an essentially male concern. Moreover, if one examines the craft from the point of view of its five essential processes – digging the clay, preparing the clay body, forming the pots, drying them and firing – then there is much evidence that the sexes co-operate in the process. Even where the craft is described as a 'female' activity because women perform the process of forming the clay into a vessel, men may co-operate in equally important tasks such as clay digging and pot firing, and in addition control the pottery trade.

The craft of pottery-making appeared late in cultural development compared with more basic techniques such as stone-working and fire-making. Yet the fact that to this day traditional potters throughout the world continue to produce their wares in great abundance and variety makes it essential that potting occupies a prominent position in our overall picture of *Man the Craftsman*. Clay is a highly plastic material which allows the creation of an almost infinite range of forms, and presents enormous opportunities for decoration. Once fired above a critical temperature, clay vessels became pottery, a substance which though fragile is extremely durable. This explains its predominance as archaeological material.

The first step in potting is to obtain clay. Although in many cases local resources are at hand, the absence of clay in the vicinity does not necessarily prevent people from making pots. Clay and other potting materials may be imported from great distances, especially where there is access to water transport. When the clay has reached the potter's home or workshop it is subjected to a lengthy process of preparation. Foreign bodies are picked out and the clay is thoroughly trampled while sand or pounded potsherd is added. The aim is to obtain a dirt-free plastic mixture of even consistency. The added substances are *fillers* which improve the working qualities of the clay-body and reduce the risk of pots exploding in firing. The next process is that of *forming,* in which pots are hand-built, using one or several of a great number of possible techniques. One of the best known of these is *coiling,* in which sausages of clay are rolled out into coils which are built one on top of the other. As the work is in progress the potter revolves the pot on some form of turntable or, alternatively, moves around the pot. After the pot is formed, it is usually smoothed and allowed to dry and harden a little before decorating. Common decorative techniques include cutting a design in the clay with a pointed implement, or impressing with a point or edge such as the thumb-nail or piece of shell. Drying often requires a period of several days and this may be followed by a pre-heating over the kitchen fire which immediately precedes firing proper. Post-firing treatment includes the application of varnish or stain to the pot while it is still hot from firing.

Many peasant folk throughout the world use the potter's wheel as well as, or instead of, hand techniques. The simple wheel of the Hindu resembles a fat cart-wheel with a clay-covered rim, and it spins in a horizontal plane on a spike in the ground; pots are thrown on a central wheel-head. Elsewhere the double or kick-wheel is used, which basically comprises two horizontal discs joined by a vertical axis and supported at the head and the bottom by bearings. In forming the pot on the wheel, or throwing, a lump of clay is literally 'thrown' onto the wheel-head. It is firmly centered, hollowed out with the thumb, and the walls drawn up with the hands, shaped, and finally smoothed off. The pot may be cut from the wheel-head with a 'cheese-wire', though oriental potters may throw several pots from each centered cone of clay.

The efficiency of some hand-made pottery techniques, especially in Mexico, compares favorably with wheel-throwing. Even in Europe, where traditional potters have for many centuries used the kick-wheel, ancient pre-wheel methods survive in many places. Gigantic wine pots several meters high are built by hand in southern Spain, for example. Each of these pots takes several months to build, and the upper part requires the use of scaffolding to complete it. In central and eastern Europe,

of the world. Potters in some areas have vigorously responded to the demand for such items as ash-trays, candle-sticks, and plant-pots as curios. In Portugal, where anthropomorphic and zoomorphic models have been made for centuries alongside utilitarian ware, the now commercialized 'Portuguese Cock' is turned out in thousands for the eager tourist. Although new external demands can create a temporary florescence in pottery methods and forms, the changes are usually associated with a decline in standards of workmanship and with a decadence of the craft as a whole.

Pottery-making, however, appears to be more resilient to such pressures in most instances than other crafts such as wood-carving and basketry, and may often remain relatively unchanged. Rather than seek for an explanation of this phenomenon in the proverbial conservatism of primitive potters, we can examine it in relation to the requirements of people who still use traditional pottery in their homes. Everyday pottery utensils generally cost no more than a few pence each – a crucial factor where the customers are poor. In India pottery is so cheap and abundant that plates and cups are sometimes treated in the same way that we use paper utensils: they are used once and thrown away. In circumstances such as this the demand for traditional ware continues and the potters comply with traditional methods.

Pottery water-coolers are used widely in the new world, in the near and far east, and in the Mediterranean region. Drinking water stored in an earthenware pot remains cool as water slowly seeps through its walls and evaporates at the outer surface. Despite the diffusion of other vessels such as the petrol-can and oil-drum, the preference for cool and sweet water in places deprived of piped water and refrigeration ensures that there is a constant demand for water-storage pots. There is also a widely expressed preference in taste for foods such as starchy puddings and meat stews cooked in pottery rather than in metal utensils, and every European gourmet appreciates the superior flavor of certain foods when they are cooked in earthenware or stoneware casseroles. These consumer preferences tend to stabilize the techniques and forms of traditional pottery making.

The aboriginal Tierra del Fuegians and Tasmanians survived into modern times possessing material cultures of extreme technical simplicity which lacked any marked degree of artistic expression. The Tasmanians lived in the crudest bark shelters, utilized rough flakes of chert (a flint-like rock) for cutting and scraping tools, and cooked in oyster shells. They made only coarse baskets, and no pottery. Such groups show that mankind in some instances survived with the barest minimum of material equipment. But they are exceptional among the vast majority of peoples of the earth who equip their homes with efficient and aesthetically attractive objects, 'luxury' goods which give them a standard of life far above that of the minimal conditions of existence.

peasants still use neolithic methods in areas associated with the old Balkan cultures.

The forms of traditional pottery are closely related to the way of life of the people who use them. Europeans are often puzzled by the preponderence of round-bottomed forms in non-European pottery. The advantage of a flat-bottomed utensil is much reduced in an environment where flat surfaces such as tables and smooth tiled or wooden floors are the exception rather than the rule. A round-bottomed vessel is also more resistant to thermal shock than one with a flat bottom, which is of great advantage in primitive pot-firing conditions or cooking over an open fire, where the sudden variations in temperature would cause other forms to shatter. The commonest way of carrying a water-pot is on the head, settled in a head-pad of grasses or of cloth: and round-bottomed forms, with their low center of gravity balance better than any other. Ceylonese women carry water-pots with the curve of the lip fitting their forearms, and the curve of the body fitting their hips and waists. A flat-bottomed pot or bucket carried in the Ceylonese manner would be most awkward. In Nigeria spherical water-pots are carried on the head, but when stood on a table or cement floor in a rich man's house, a woven pot-ring is used to support the vessel in an upright position.

As we all know, once remote parts of the world are being increasingly brought into contact with the modern world. What are the effects of this process on the craft of pottery-making? Mass-produced plastic and metal wares are replacing traditional ceramic utensils in some parts

33

# Man the home-maker

This beautiful chest comes from mid-14th century Egypt. It is a container for the holy Koran, and is made of bronze with Islamic inscriptions inlaid in silver.

In a village in Galilee, Israel, a Beduin woman grinds corn the traditional way, between two round, flat stones.

Intricately carved from wood and elaborately inlaid with tortoise shell and mother-of-pearl, tables like this are prize possessions in many Arab homes. Some have an inlaid chess or backgammon board, others are used as coffee tables. The hookah is of carved brass with a colorful snake-like smoking pipe.

The Sagaja are locally famous for their brandy made by their own special method.

In central Asia many tribes carve utensils from tree bark. Some, like this one, are also carefully decorated.

In many parts of the world the staple food is flat unleavened bread. From the heat of the Sahara to the snowy wastes of Siberia it is baked in round stone ovens. This Evenki woman has just chopped wood to light the fire

## Southern Asia

The craft of basket making is one of the earliest and most widespread. Used mainly for storing and gathering, some clay-lined varieties can also be used for cooking.

The water-pipe, hookah or *nargileh* is found in many places, mainly in Asia and northern Africa. Some are filled with plain water, but rose water is very popular for a more luxurious smoke.

This Senoi girl of the Malay peninsula takes a long drink of fresh spring water. Each day the women of her village carry several bamboo nodes like this one from the river to their homes.

## Western-dominated world

For centuries food was cooked over open fires and in stoves with wood or coal fires underneath them. Later these were supplemented by small oil stoves and a variety of other implements, but no modern housewife today would consider parting with her convenient new cooker, be it gas or electric.

In the wine-making monasteries of Mount Athos, in Greece, urns like this one are used to store and mature the wine.

The western flush WC has recently come under severe criticism for causing waste of precious water. Research is under way for a new chemical WC to replace it.

# Man the home-maker

One of man's earliest weapons was the club. Though he probably used animal bones at first, clubs fashioned from wood were soon developed.

In Arnhemland, Australia, a man drinks thirstily from a traditional palm-leaf container. The handle is made from another leaf cleverly folded.

A craftsman in Cameroun fashions mortars from thick tree trunks.

In many countries breadfruit is a staple food. This implement is specially designed to split breadfruit. Its actual length is 40 cm.

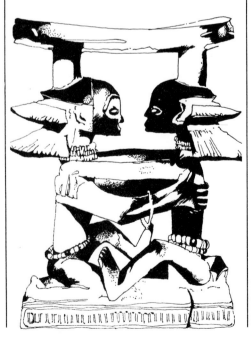

From Zaïre, formerly Congo Kinshasa, comes this piece of tribal sculpture. It is a head rest supported by a pair of women wrestling, and its actual size is 17 cm.

Although most household tools and implements are strictly utilitarian in design and appearance, some are beautifully decorated. This spatula comes from Australia and is about 25 cm long.

## Amerindia

The Yanomamo people keep their food safe from water and animals on special food-racks like this construction of leather and wood.

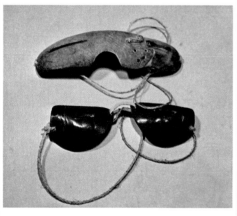

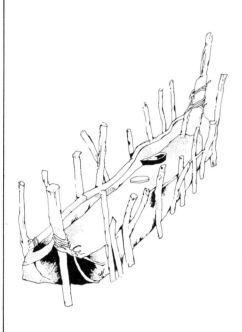

The Eskimo have always needed protection from the glare of the snow; without it they would soon become blind. In the past they wore wooden goggles with narrow slits. Today modern science has helped them with the invention of dark lenses.

The *ulu* is about 12·5 cm long. It has a wide blade of copper and a handle carved from ivory or bone. Eskimo women use it to scrape and clean sealskins.

## Orient

Rice paper lampshades originated in the far east; they give a soft and pleasant light and have become popular in the west as well.

One of the less common uses of the basket is when it is attached to a yoke: in this case filled with geese going to market.

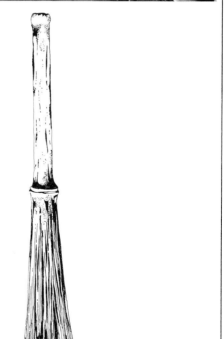

The versatility of bamboo is well illustrated by this simple but effective broom: the top half is a handle, the bottom is finely shredded for sweeping. It is about 125 cm long.

# Man the home-maker

Pounding grain is an alternative to milling it. This Nemadi woman throws her pounding pole in the air, aiming it accurately so that it will land in the mortar.

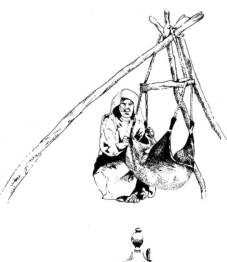

Shepherds the world over use different methods for churning their milk into butter. Nomads of the Arabian and Sahara deserts use goatskin bags suspended from poles.

The Arab likes his coffee very thick, hot and sweet. This brass coffee pot will be kept simmering for hours until the owner is ready for a cup.

Tea is a drink of infinite variety; some, like the Mongolians, actually eat it, having made it into a thick soup by adding butter, milk and gruel. The Russians make tea in a samovar in which the flavor depends on the kind of leaves that are put in the cylinder.

The Ket of Siberia have to make the most of the short summer when fish are abundant. They use special nets and weirs which direct the fish into an enclosed area where they can be speared easily.

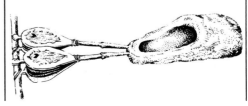

In Siberia this clay kiln is used for making crude pots; blacksmiths' bellows are an integral part of the kiln.

## Southern Asia

*Papier-mâché* is a useful substance for mainly decorative implements like this pretty box from south-east Asia.

This Balinese is cooking *sate*, chopped meat and spices, on a bamboo stick over a coconut-shell fire. The food is to be offered to the gods and later eaten by the villagers.

The craft of pottery making is a relatively late development, but has come to occupy a very prominent position. The creative part is the actual forming of the pot, but the more technical processes take time and effort.

## Western-dominated world

The four-poster bed was once the height of luxury and prestige, only within the reach of the very wealthy. Thick curtains drawn round the bed gave privacy and kept out the night air which was believed to be harmful.

Created by Thomas Tompion (1671-1713) this 8-day striking and repeating English bracket clock is 35 cm high and is valued at $55,000

Crystal chandeliers were once a symbol of wealth and status. Smaller versions are sold today, but the trend has recently been towards simpler, sparer designs.

# Man the home-maker

Raffia is easy to dye and raffian baskets tend to be more colorful and decorative than straw and bamboo ones.

Though it may look fragile and thin, a well-made raffia bed can easily sleep a full-grown man.

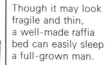

East African women bring the results of long hours at the wheel and kiln to sell at a local market.

Kava is the favorite drink of Melanesia an it is mildly intoxicatin King Thakombau of Fiji owned this large (105 cm) Kava bowl

The village of Aibom in New Guinea is famed for its pottery. In each communal hu there are several ceramic fireplaces, or to each family, where villagers dry their fish Dried fish, stored in the bucket with sago is their staple food.

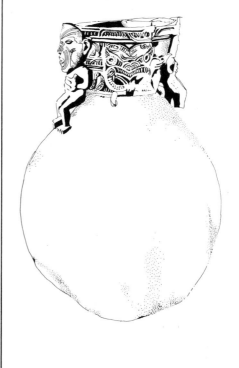

This container is a unique Maori gourc The body is plain and functional but the neck is beautifully intricate. The figures are those of ancestors and other famous tribal figures.

## Amerindia

Keeping flies and mosquitoes off young babies calls for ingenious inventions like this net-covered baby board used by Indians in Arizona.

The Eskimo bow-drill is used to make fire by friction and also to drill holes in wood and bone. It is useful in the manufacture of other implements.

The most versatile of all beds, the hammock can be put up between two trees, indoors or out. As it is almost impossible to fall out of, it has long been used on board ships.

## Orient

This fine carved Tz'u Chou pillow, shaped like a bean, is 25 cm across and is of the Sung dynasty period of Chinese ceramics.

In many ways chopsticks are far superior to western cutlery as eating implements. They are lighter, easier to clean and cheap to replace.

A 50 cm high ceramic pilgrim flask of the Ch'ien Lung period illustrates the fine art of the Chinese craftsmen of the 15th century.

43

# Man the food-getter

Providing food is a basic necessity of human life. Every individual member of society needs enough food to keep his body alive and healthy – although exactly what his nutritional requirements are is a matter of some controversy. Basic nutritional requirements vary according to an individual's age, his type of work and his other activities. A professional footballer will need a different type of diet to a typist who spends all day sitting in an office chair. Physiological factors also affect the type of food an individual needs. A baby, an invalid or an old man can digest only certain types of food.

In an ideal world each person would receive food according to his physiological or dietary requirements, and would have enough to keep his body functioning healthily. But the world is far from ideal. While many people in the developed western world eat far more than they need and suffer diseases as a consequence of over-eating, people in other parts of the world have too little food and suffer the diseases of malnutrition.

It would be wrong, however, to see food simply in terms of satisfying nutritional needs. Eating food is also a cultural activity. The cultural aspect of food can be seen in simple terms as the body of ideas which each generation inherits about the type of food it can eat, the appropriate time to eat it and the right way to cook and prepare it. These ideas vary from society to society. Eating snails and reptiles, for example, may be considered a luxury in some societies and abhorred in others. In some cultures eating certain animals may be forbidden by religious taboos: the Hindu taboo on eating beef and the Muslim taboo on pork are two examples. There are similar differences in the way people choose to prepare food; in whether a particular plant is cooked or eaten raw, for example, or eaten by itself or mixed with other vegetables. Such cultural factors need not conflict in any way with the satisfaction of our nutritional requirements. What is essential is that a compromise is struck between what we like to eat and what our culture allows us to eat on the one hand and what we need simply for survival on the other.

Man's nutritional requirements can be satisfied by an almost infinite variety of foods of different types. And the ways in which food plants and animals are obtained are equally varied. Food is the product of the natural environment. But getting it is modified by man's cultural ideas and technical actions. There is a wide range of options in most parts of the world and, given sufficient technical knowledge, the resources of any environment can be used in a number of different ways. In certain parts of the world climatic and environmental conditions limit the possibilities more than in others. The frozen wastes of the Arctic and the arid desert areas, for example, provide comparatively few alternative food resources. Even in these environments people do not use all the food resources that are available to them. The plants and animals which the indigenous peoples of these areas

choose for food reflect their cultural choices. Of all the edible plants of the Australian desert, for example, only some are selected as food, and the selection will vary from tribe to tribe.

The methods man uses to obtain food can be broadly divided as follows: hunting and gathering, pastoralism and agriculture. These categories of food getting are not mutually exclusive. People may be both cultivators and hunters as is the case with many New Guinea societies, or pastoralists and gatherers like the Lapps. Moreover these different methods of obtaining food do not represent stages in an evolutionary sequence. When the horse was introduced to North America, for example, several Indian tribes who had previously been agriculturalists changed to buffalo hunting for their main source of food. Although it is reasonable to suppose that man's forefathers were originally hunter-gatherers, there is as yet no substantial evidence that plants were domesticated before animals or vice-versa.

It is wrong to assume that in hunter-gatherer societies food is simply collected at random from trees and bushes or obtained by killing animals that just happen to be around. This is far from the truth. The degree of technical

knowledge hunter-gatherers require to obtain food has been dramatically demonstrated on many occasions by the inability of early European explorers to survive in areas which provide ample support for their indigenous populations. Many early expeditions into the center of Australia – for example the Burke and Wills expedition – ended in tragedy through failure to use the food resources of the desert.

Survival depends on a detailed knowledge of the distribution of vegetation and water resources and on knowledge of the distribution and habits of the birds and animals. Lures are one means by which the intimate knowledge of the behavior and habitat of birds and animals can be used in hunting them. When the Blackfoot Indians sight a herd of buffalo a man dressed in skins wearing a buffalo head mask attracts the attention of the

44

At lotus-harvest time in Te-min-hu in China, naked men stand in the shallow water feeling with their toes for the roots of lotus plants.

herd and lures them towards a pound on the top of a cliff. Once the herd is inside the pound the other members of the tribe cause it to stampede headlong over the clifftop, killing the majority of the animals. This method of hunting may appear wasteful and there is indeed a danger that hunting any species of animal exclusively may lead to its extinction. By their traditional methods the Blackfoot and other Plains Indians did little to alter the overall size of the herds. On the other hand the indiscriminate slaughter of herds by white hunters using guns led in a few short years to the almost total disappearance of the buffalo.

Not only do people in hunter-gatherer societies have to learn to hunt. They must also learn to make the best possible use of scarce resources. They must ensure both an equitable distribution of game and that supplies will last throughout the year. They may do this by preserving the foods they obtain in times of abundance to use in time of scarcity. The north-west coast American Indians, for example, preserved the salmon they caught during the spring and summer by smoking them, and the berries they gathered by drying them and making them into cakes. In this way they had ample supplies to last them the winter months.

Hunter-gatherer communities must be as careful to conserve their environment and avoid over-exploiting it as most farming communities. Conservation is by no means a new idea. Australian Aborigines, for example, who live in the Simpson desert north of Lake Eyre, were forced to spend most of the year concentrated around the few semi-permanent waterholes which could support life during the long periods of drought. As soon as the winter rains fell the Aborigines would break camp and move out into the surrounding desert region to allow the flora and fauna of these waterholes to regenerate.

For many years it was assumed that hunter-gatherers could scratch but a meager living from the land. It was assumed that pastoralism and agriculture were stages that must necessarily be passed through before people could develop elaborate cultural patterns. Hunter-gathering was seen as an occupation that involved endless hard labor for mere subsistence returns. No one, it was assumed, would be a hunter-gatherer of choice. A man would only be a hunter-gatherer because he had not developed the technical resources that would have enabled him to reach the better life through agriculture. Recently it has been realized that this picture of the hunter-gatherer is far from the truth. Most hunter-gatherers spend only a small proportion of their time obtaining food; the rest of the time they spend engaged in a wide range of socio-cultural activities.

A second fallacy is that as all hunter-gatherers spend most of their time wandering from place to place in search of food they cannot establish permanent camps. In certain areas their movements may be fairly constant (for example in much of aboriginal Australia) but in other areas the abundance of food combined with their knowledge of techniques of preserving it, enables them to form relatively large permanent or semi-permanent villages. The north-west coast American Indians, for example, have permanent villages of a number of large cedar buildings, each of which houses a number of related families. These may, as among the coastal Salish, have a total population of over 100.

The equipment used by hunter-gatherers varies according to a number of factors: the variety, type and abundance of food resources, for example, the topography of the area, the raw materials available and the techniques which the hunters use. The Aborigines of the Australian desert, for example, spend much of their time moving from one campsite to another in search of food and water. This continuous movement in harsh ecological conditions means that the group must keep their material possessions to a minimum, to what is sufficient to obtain and prepare food but does not hamper the group's progress. There is an emphasis on multifunctional implements which, with certain modifications, can be adapted for a variety of purposes. A boomerang, for example, will be used not only as a throwing implement, but also as a digging stick for uprooting plants and tubers, as a musical instrument (by clapping two boomerangs together) and as a handle to which stone tools can be attached by resin to form a variety of different cutting tools.

Eskimo, who live in an equally harsh though very different environment to the Australian Aborigines, have similarly been forced to adapt to the constraints imposed on them by their environment. During the long winter months the Eskimo move camp to the shores where they depend almost entirely for food and raw materials on hunting a single animal, the seal, which provides meat for eating and blubber for heating. During the short summer months the Eskimo are freed from the strictures of their environment and have a wider range of economic activities: hunting caribou and musk ox, fishing for salmon and collecting berries. During this period surplus meat and fish are preserved to supplement their winter diet, and caribou skins provide them with the clothing that they need to survive the extreme cold of the Arctic winter. The lack of trees in their environment means that the majority of their objects are made from animal products, although during the summer they sometimes find driftwood which they can use. The Eskimo make an extremely wide variety of material objects using the limited materials at their disposal – harpoons, spears, spear throwers, bows and arrows, kayaks – and because they use dog sleds they can transport these things over considerable distances without affecting their mobility. Their climate is so severe, however, that much of this equipment has to be jettisoned at the onset of winter and replaced each summer.

Pastoralism is a term that is usually reserved for economies which depend primarily for their food on 45 exploiting domesticated animals. The advantage that a pastoral economy has over a hunting economy is that man can maintain control over his livestock. By restricting their movement he can keep livestock within easy access of the settlement site. And by controlling the feeding and growth of his herds the pastoralist can ensure a continuous supply of food throughout the year. These advantages apply particularly in areas of the world where herds of wild animals are scarce and widely scattered. Many pastoralists do however supplement their diet by hunting wild game, gathering berries and so on. The Tungus of Siberia, for example, exploit domesticated herds of reindeer while at the same time hunting wild reindeer and other animals.

There are pastoralist economies in many parts of the world, in a wide variety of ecological zones. The majority of these areas can be linked by certain characteristics – the absence of dense forest, for example, and a moderate to low rainfall – though there are exceptions. The species of animal that can be exploited varies according to the environment. In certain parts of the world the pastoralist has very little choice as only certain species can survive. The Beduin tribes of the Arabian desert depend almost entirely on the camel both as a beast of burden and as a provider of food, as no other animal capable of supporting man can survive the long stretches without water. The reindeer is similarly vital to the pastoral economies of northern Europe and Asia as it can live off the lichen and sparse vegetation of the area. In areas of richer pasture, such as the forest margin regions of Asia and the savanna grasslands of Africa, it is possible to herd a greater range of domesticated animals, although usually only a single species of animal forms the main basis of the economy to the exclusion of others.

The majority of pastoralists are migratory. In order to obtain sufficient grazing land throughout the year they must spend much of their time on the move. Their movements are generally highly systematized; the best pastures are well known and herdsmen move their animals between them. The Masai, for example, will continually return to and reconstruct their main kraals (cattle compounds), leaving them when the available pasture has been fully exploited and returning to them when the grassland has regenerated. Pasture is sometimes rich enough for fairly permanent villages to be set up in which the pastoralists may lead a semi-sedentary existence. The Kalmuck of the Altai mountains of south-west China are able to establish semi-permanent villages in sheltered areas where rich grass supports their sheep and horses throughout the year within reach of the settlement. This way of life is, however, the exception rather than the rule for pastoralists.

As whole communities of pastoralists must be able to move considerable distances at short notice the equipment they carry must, if it is not to be abandoned, be light and portable. But although the pastoralists' herds force them to move they also provide them with the means to move people and household goods. The *yurt* dwelling of the Kirghiz of Turkistan is an excellent example. The frame of the *yurt* consists of a number of collapsible trellises of wood bound with leather, which is then covered with sheets of felt. When camp is moved the *yurt* is dismantled and the parts carried by a number of pack horses or camels.

The majority of the world's population depends for at least part of its diet on agriculture, although many agriculturalists supplement their diet by hunting and gathering. Western European agricultural economies, for example, obtain much of their protein requirements through fishing. Agriculture can be defined as the actual cultivation of plants by collecting seeds and planting them in cleared land as opposed to the collection of naturally grown products. There is a vast number of different types of agricultural economies in the world. They can be divided into two broad types: shifting agriculture and sedentary agriculture. This distinction refers to differences in the ways land is used rather than settlement patterns.

According to one definition (by Pelzeu), shifting agriculture is an economy of which the main characteristics are the rotation of fields rather than crops. Shifting agriculturalists first clear an area of land with axes and knives and may burn the brushwood. They then plant crops, usually for a period of one to three years, until the fertility of the soil is exhausted, after which they move on to repeat the process in another place, allowing the fertility of the soil to be restored by the regeneration of the natural vegetation. The same places may be resorted to again and again after a certain period of time has elapsed, the length of the cycle depending on the fertility of the soil and the cultivation techniques.

Shifting agriculturalists may move their settlement each year they make a new clearing – as do the Boro of the Amazon basin. Villages may, on the other hand, be semi-permanent. Every few years a new clearing may be made for cultivation within easy access of the settlement site, as is the case in the Yucatan region of southern Mexico. The permanency of the settlement and the population density of an area under shifting agriculture depends on a number of factors: the fertility of the soil, the speed with which fallow land regenerates, the variety and type of crops that are grown and the agricultural implements that are available. The great Mayan civilization of Central America supported an estimated 60 persons per square kilometer, by a system of slash-and-burn shifting agriculture similar to that practised in parts of the region to this day. In Zambia, on the other hand, it has been estimated that the maximum population density that could be supported by slash-and-burn techniques was 8 persons per square kilometer. There are similar variations in the number of different crops which shifting agriculturalists grow. In much of Melanesia the economy

46

In a field near Memphis, Egypt, an Archimedes screw is used to bring water up to a higher level.

depends on producing a single crop, the yam. The Hananvo, at the opposite extreme, grow as many as 280 different crops.

Sedentary agriculture can be defined as agriculture which depends on the continuous exploitation of the same area of land over long periods of time. Sedentary farmers have a number of alternative ways of maintaining fertility. One way is by rotating crops. Crop rotation depends on the fact that certain plants use different minerals in the soil to others, also on the fact that some plants produce minerals which can be used by other plants. By annually rotating carefully selected plants it is possible to maintain the balance of minerals in the soil and its level of fertility. There are many different systems of crop rotation. Some of them may involve leaving a certain number of fields fallow for one or two years. A second method of maintaining fertility is by adding vital minerals to the soil each year, either by using artificial fertilizer, animal manures or plant compost. A third technique is by replacing the soil itself. In Lower Egypt, before the Aswan dam was built, the natural forces of the Nile were harnessed by man to perform this task for him. In this case the annual flooding of the Nile brought a new layer of silt. By controlling the extent of the flood over field systems both the water content and the mineral content of the soil were maintained.

The advantage of settled agriculture over shifting agriculture is that a higher population density can be supported by ensuring a greater use of land resources. Settled agriculture, however, generally requires more labor to expand it so as to produce similar returns. Thus it is quite conceivable that where there is no pressure on land resources shifting agriculture might be practised in preference to sedentary agriculture. This could be the case in much of black Africa. Although knowledge of the techniques of settled agriculture is widespread in Africa some of the most intensive agriculture in the world is practised by the people of Ukana Island in Lake Tanganyika who prefer the system of shifting agriculture.

The type of land that can be cultivated and the population size that it can support also depends to a considerable extent on the technical systems used to cultivate it. Over much of the world subsistence agriculture is successfully practised on good soils with a minimum amount of technical equipment. Often the tools used by hunter-gatherers, axes, knives and a digging stick, will be enough to produce an adequate supply of food by agriculture. For more intensive agriculture, and especially farming on heavy clay soils, plows are often necessary to loosen and turn the soil. Different types of plow, with or without the use of draft animals, have different effects; some merely scratch the surface of the soil whereas others dig deeply into it. The plow is useful either for shifting or for settled agriculture. In some dry areas of the world agriculture can only be practised in conjunction with a system of irrigation which takes water from a particular source, a

river, lake or well, and distributes it through channels over a wide area. The equipment used for irrigation can vary enormously in complexity, but invariably it requires co-operation between the individuals who own the water sources and the people who use the water.

The need to obtain food and the way in which food is obtained impose constraints on people's lives without determining the form their lives take. The religious beliefs of hunter-gatherers, for example, differ widely from group to group. They are no more nor less comparable with one another than they are with the beliefs of groups who are not hunter-gatherers. All societies are in a state of continual change that is generated by both internal and external factors. Change in the economic circumstances of people's lives will have an effect on other aspects of their culture. There is no internal reason why primitive societies could not adapt to the changing circumstances brought about by contact with western forms of life. Tragically, the internal mechanisms by which they could adapt to innovation have often been inhibited or prohibited by externally imposed legal constraints based on the rigid preconceptions of social order held by the colonial intruders.

(Over page) Harmful insects used to destroy banana crops in Central America. Today insecticides are sprayed from the air.

# Man the food-getter

In Pakistan the wooden plow and the ox do most of the agricultural work in the fields.

In Tunisia the camel often replaces the ox as draft animal. For generations the peasant has struggled to make his living from the arid, stony and infertile soil.

On the outskirts of Herat in Afghanistan a professional pumper works all day for a subsistence wage. Electric power only comes on at night.

In central Asia these ski-like implements are used as grain threshers; they are pulled over the grain by cows or oxen and the chaff blows out through the holes.

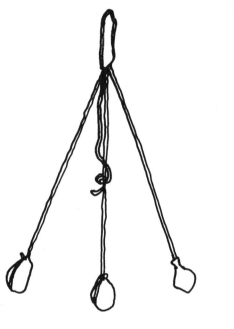

The people of Siberia use this device for hunting birds. It is much like an ordinary sling, except that the stones are tied to a central loop. It is about 7.5 cm long.

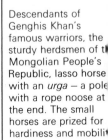

Descendants of Genghis Khan's famous warriors, the sturdy herdsmen of the Mongolian People's Republic, lasso horses with an *urga* – a pole with a rope noose at the end. The small horses are prized for hardiness and mobility and are a sign of wealth.

## Southern Asia

In central India axes like these are used to cut and chop wood for building and for firewood.

In Vietnam peasants winnow the rice to separate the chaff from the grain. This is done from hand-held basins.

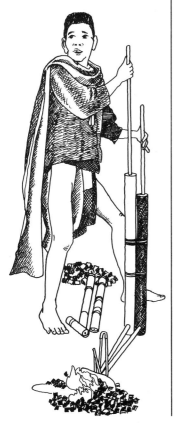

A Jeh blacksmith's assistant in the village of Dak Jel Luk in Vietnam keeps the fire hot by pumping air onto it. The different widths of pipe create the necessary pressure. The primitive Vulcan will then hammer the hot metal into the tools he needs.

## Western-dominated world

In Connemara, Ireland, harvesting is done by hand. The combine-harvesters and tractors have not yet replaced the laborer and his scythe.

The members of the 'Utopia Club' in America make it their purpose to increase farm yields year after year. Russell Lawson's project is to improve crops of dark tobacco.

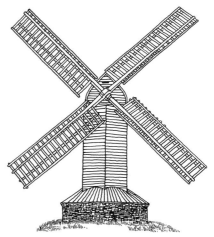

The sails of the windmill are beginning to regain their past importance: as fuel shortages reach crisis point, wind- and water-powered machinery is appreciated for more than its aesthetic value.

# Man the food-getter

In Ethiopia cows walk round and round on the threshing circle, with blinkers on their eyes to preserve their sanity. This method has been in use since biblical times.

The simplest method of winnowing grain is to pour it out of its container when a wind or breeze is blowing. The lightweight chaff blows away, and the heavier grain falls on a heap at the girl's feet. This is how it is done in Madagascar.

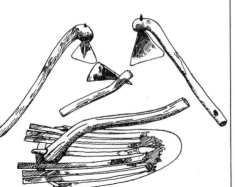

The natives of Nigeria use these simply constructed but effective axes for wood chopping and cultivation.

In central New Guine a woman plants sweet potatoes. First she makes a deep ho in the soft earth with her stick, then puts t young plants in, and covers them, using t same stick.

The Aborigines of Australia grind seeds between round ston in the ancient way. I a household craft ea mother teaches her daughters at a young age.

The pandanus leaf o the Ellice Islands ha many uses: the islan women make mats from it and weave th traditional costumes, the men thatch hous with it. The dried lea is used for rolling tobacco into the loc cigarettes.

## Amerindia

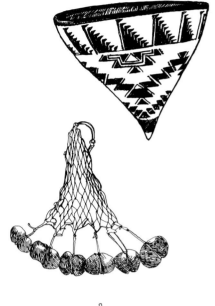

A typical Indian twined basket from the Pitt river. The shape is conical and the design is black on a white background.

The Indians and Eskimo of North America hunted birds with this *bolas*: the net with the stone weights was thrown among them and a few birds were inevitably caught in it.

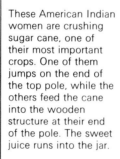

These American Indian women are crushing sugar cane, one of their most important crops. One of them jumps on the end of the top pole, while the others feed the cane into the wooden structure at their end of the pole. The sweet juice runs into the jar.

Hunting on the ice, this Eskimo seal hunter carries a white screen as well as his rifle so that he can get very near to his unsuspecting prey without being seen.

## Orient

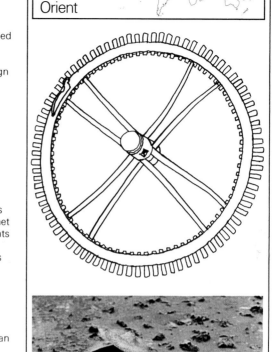

This wheel is an animal-powered irrigation apparatus used in China. It is made entirely of hard wood, and 210 cm in diameter. A rope fastens the wheel to the animal's nose bolt, keeping its head inclined towards the wheel so that it will walk around it for hours without guidance.

The water buffalo is a useful animal for draft and labor. It is especially suitable for plowing in flooded paddy fields.

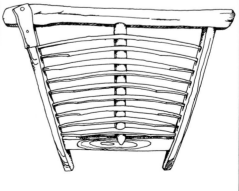

The Chinese threshing frame is 108 cm wide at the top and 80 cm long. The slats are 42 cm thick and are made of a harder wood than the frame itself. The sheaves are struck against it and the heavy grain accumulates on the other side.

# Man the food-getter

A primitive water-drawing structure, curiously similar to the more solid wells of medieval Europe. The principle is simply that of a bucket on a long rope which can be lowered into the water and raised again.

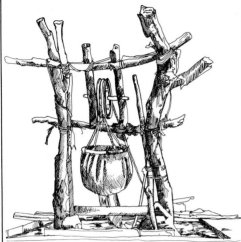

Throughout the steaming summer these dates are carefully tended on Ha'on *kibbutz* in Israel. They are harvested in mid-October when they are at the peak of ripeness and sweetness. In Hebrew the word for 'honey' also means 'dates'.

Camel caravans constantly transport salt across hundreds of miles from the bed at Bilma oasis to markets in southern Niger. At Bilma workers pour water into potholes. The water absorbs the salt from the earth and when it evaporates a layer of salt crystals remains, which is easy to collect.

A Georgian shepherd guides his flocks across the Krestov pass in the Caucasus.

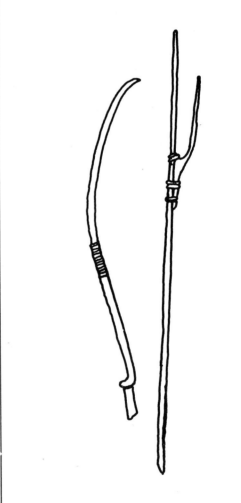

In central Asia the hump-backed scythe still in use for harvesting. Haystacks are made with crude wooden pitch-forks.

The Kalash Kafir of north-west Pakistan have a complex system of rules for the rotation of the limited water supplies to their irrigated hill terraces and valley fields.

## Southern Asia

The balance net is used in Vietnam for fishing. Boiled rice is thrown into the net as bait before it is lowered into the water.

On Lake Inle in Burma this fisherman propels his boat by the leg-rowing method: he stands on the edge of the boat on one leg, and his other, his most powerful limb, is on the oar which is contoured to the shape of a leg.

This man in Madras is an expert and experienced tree climber. With the tools of his trade he seeks coconuts, the milk from which is made into a powerful alcoholic drink.

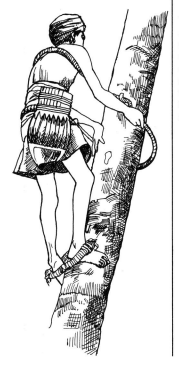

## Western-dominated world

The modern combine harvester was built to reduce the manpower which was once essential to agricultural work. It is with the aid of machines like this that the United States produces more grain than any other country though a mere 5% of its population are farmers.

The windmills of Mikonos in Greece have sails designed to take best advantage of the prevailing winds.

There are about 600 vineyards within the urban area of Vienna. Many of the vintners mingle different varieties of grape in a single plot to assure each grower a distinctive and unique wine.

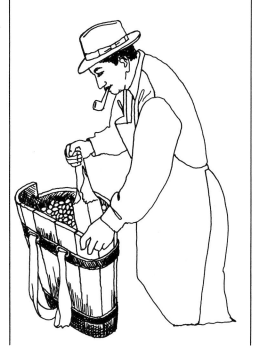

In north Cameroun a Hausa man fishes on the River Benue. The net is lowered into the water every few minutes then raised to a vertical position. Small fish then slide into a basket tray near the bottom.

A woman of the Okavango is using a dip trap to fish. The fish she catches will be dried and pounded to a powder and used to flavor the rice porridge which is the area's staple food.

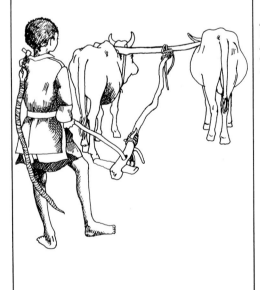

Among the cattle-breeding tribes of Africa, like the Baggara, oxen are used as draft animals.

Lakemba Island women from Fiji fish the lagoon using semi circular nets made of coconut fiber string. Their faces are blackened to prevent sun-tan, as fair skin is socially desirable.

The Dayak of Borneo use the scissor principle for fishing: the net is lowered into the water in the open position, and is closed on the fish when they swim into it.

Trapping birds with a net is a long established practice on the Ellice Islands. It requires both skill and patience. The birds nest on the tops of coconut trees and are caught, often in large numbers, when feeding their young or at night, when they are asleep.

## Amerindia

## Orient

The Nootka Indians of Cape Flattery in Washington State use elaborate fish-hooks: the wooden hooks have bone barbs and are decorated with colored string. Even more luxurious ones are made of mother-of-pearl.

This is a fishing comb. It has a long wooden handle for a good grip with both hands; the patient fisherman squats motionless in a clear shallow stream until he sees the fish stopped by his device.

In a small lake in Wu-hsi, in China, fishermen use large conical shaped nets to trap their catch.

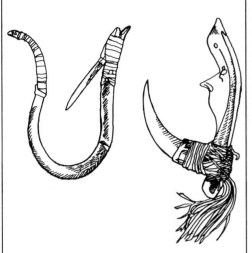

Mestizo fishermen of Cienaga Grande throw their nets into sea-water lakes on the Caribbean coast of north Colombia. The fish are later sold in the nearby port of Barranquilla.

Chinese peasants in the northern Hunan province use this primitive roller with its three stone wheels to level the soil after sowing the grain.

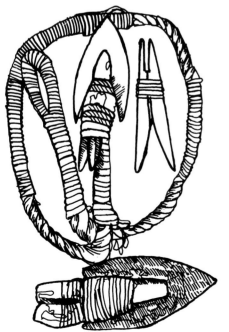

A North American Makah Indian whale harpoon, made of three components, has a pair of barbs, two complete spurs with copper or iron blades and a rope.

# Man attired

Arab tribesmen keep their possessions in padlocked leather pouches. Their women tie the keys to their long flowing veils for safety.

It is, of course, basically true that man clothes himself in order to keep warm or cool or as protection from dust, insects or thorns. The thick padded garments, heavy boots and fur hats worn in Tibet and Mongolia during the severe winter are clearly adaptations to climate. And the loose flowing cotton robe and head-cloth worn by men in Saudi Arabia provides suitable protection against sun and dust.

But a comparative study of the costumes of different peoples in relation to their environment reveals that the protective function of clothing is not a sufficient explanation of why man wears clothes. There are indeed certain parts of the world such as the extreme north of America and Asia where warm clothing is essential for survival in the intense cold, but there are also areas where people submit to considerable physical discomfort by failing to wear adequate covering. The primitive Ona of Tierra del Fuego, for example, suffer a cold wet climate and frequently experience sub-zero temperatures, yet their garments consist of no more than a loin cloth and a loose cape of guanaco, seal or otter skin and they otherwise protect themselves from the cold only by coating their bodies with grease and clay. In the semi-desert environment of the Australian Aborigines high daytime temperatures drop sharply during the night when the Aborigines sleep so close to the embers of the campfire that they scorch their skin, yet despite the availability of furbearing animals, they mostly wear no clothing. Even in western society a considerable degree of discomfort is sometimes regarded as acceptable and women will wear unsuitable clothing such as short skirts and nylon stockings in sub-zero weather.

There are, as well as the protective function, many other equally significant motives for wearing clothes. There are, particularly, socially and culturally conditioned criteria: the advertising of age, for example, status, or of wealth or occupation; and there are standards of modesty, as well as the universal human desire for adornment and display.

A striking illustration of the way in which costume can be used to indicate status or rank is the brilliant dress of the former Chinese court, which reflected a carefully organized hierarchy within the society of the time. The main decorative theme of Chinese court robes linked motifs of dragons among clouds, rocks and waves with cosmic symbolism, and regulations were published in elaborate volumes prescribing the colors and decorations, including seasonal variations, which were permitted for the various ranks of members of the court from the Emperor downwards.

The marks of kingship frequently incorporate materials of special rarity to emphasize the wearer's high rank. The Shahs of Persia on ceremonial occasions glitter with a wealth of precious jewels. In the Hawaiian Islands, prior to European contact, the chiefs and nobility wore vivid cloaks and headdresses covered with the tiny red and

CLEFS DE VOILE

yellow breast feathers of certain types of parakeet. The birds were caught live and only a few feathers removed before they were released again. Many thousands of feathers went into the manufacture of a single cloak.

This visible definition of social hierarchy by means of costume has an obvious parallel in military uniform. In North America the war leaders of certain tribes of Plains Indians wore feather bonnets as a mark of honor and leadership. East African Masai society is based on a carefully graded military organization divided into various ranks of junior and senior warriors. The warriors are distinguished from uninitiated boys who have not passed into the junior grade and from elders or retired warriors by arm clamps and other special ornaments and spectacular headdresses of ostrich feathers and lion's manes. Carefully detailed military uniforms are a feature of European rather than oriental armies although during the 19th century the Persian and Ottoman Empires adopted uniforms based on European examples.

Wearing a special costume or uniform by which a person's occupation or profession is immediately apparent is a widespread practice. Examples in western society are postmen, policemen and nurses whose uniforms are both practical and make it easier to identify their role instantly. In traditional Japanese society the courtesan, and the geisha – whose role was a professional hostess-entertainer, an occupation without parallel in the west – were recognized by special costumes. The courtesan dressed conspicuously, using brilliant colored materials for her kimono and obi, or sash, and wearing an elaborate sculptured coiffure bristling with jeweled pins. She was a leader of fashion and wore styles which other women might secretly admire but dared not imitate. The geisha, although less flamboyant, was nevertheless meticulously groomed, and wore special patterns for her kimono and obi which immediately identified her profession.

Details of costume and ornament are also used to signify differences in age and marital status. Married women are distinguised from single girls by certain marks which range from a simple finger-ring in western society to more dramatic signs among other peoples. In parts of south-east Nigeria Ibo girls have their heads completely shaven on their first offer of marriage, which may be at quite an early age, and in some areas they go naked until their wedding day when they don a wrap-over cotton skirt. Among certain groups alterations in marital status, or even the desire for alteration, are indicated by complicated signals involving colors and accessories. A Yuruk nomad girl from Turkey borders her silk head-scarf with gold coins to show that she is ready for marriage. On betrothal she will add a white silk scarf to show that she is promised. A Yuruk widow will place a black silk scarf over plaited hair if she wishes to remarry, but if she prefers to remain a widow she will leave her hair loose beneath the scarf.

Costume may be used to define other ceremonial occasions within a society besides engagement and marriage, such as coming of age, and mourning, and many of these events may have a religious significance to the people concerned. In all societies those individuals who bear special responsibility for communicating with the spiritual world are distinguished by special costume and accessories. These may be as simple as the 'dog collar' of Protestant ministers, or as lavish as the vestments of Roman Catholic and Orthodox clergy. The garments themselves often have a complex religious symbolism. The cloak of a Buddhist priest, though often made of rich fabric, for ceremonies always has a patched pattern symbolizing the Buddhist vows of humility and poverty, because originally the monks collected cast-off rags, washed them and sewed them together to make cloaks. The costume of the Muslim order of Mevlevi dervishes embodies imagery symbolic of death and spiritual rebirth. Dervish dancers wear caps of camel wool representing tombstones and white robes representing shrouds, covered by black cloaks to symbolize the shedding of wordly cares and emergence from the grave.

Religious ideas are so frequently intermingled with social customs that the primary motivation is often difficult to determine. The origin of the custom of seclusion and veiling of women, traditionally associated with Muslim countries, is ambiguous. The Koran recommends that women behave with suitable modesty, but does not specifically mention seclusion. Possibly the tradition may be explained in terms of a socially-dictated modesty with which the general principles of Muslim religion did not conflict. The outdoor costume of Muslim women, consisting of an enveloping garment which provides the wearer with a portable form of seclusion, dramatically demonstrates this extreme modesty. The degree of concealment in Muslim countries varied and still does vary from place to place, and is more marked in the towns than in rural areas where economic necessity obliges the peasant woman to undertake a more active working life. In Afghanistan and parts of Pakistan townswomen wear the *chaudri* a voluminous pleated

tent suspended from a pillbox cap with an embroidered lattice at eye level. But this is a streamlined garment compared with the cumbersome three-piece costume of horsehair visor, cap and cloak worn by the women of Bokhara. At the other extreme, in some north African Muslim groups, women veil their faces although their breasts are bare.

Standards of modesty are socially determined and vary enormously from one society to another. Apart from a skin skirt and a profusion of ornaments, a married Masai woman regards her nakedness as normal, but she will be overcome with shame if anyone, even her husband, should see her without the special brass earrings which are a mark of her married status. The Eskimo who are among the most completely covered people in the world, outside their own dwellings, will undress almost entirely once they are within their warm houses, despite the presence of strangers or guests. In New Guinea the men of certain tribes expose the testicles but encase the penis in a gourd sheath which, they feel, it is immodest to remove in public. In western society the degree of bodily exposure that is considered acceptable varies with the occasion. A bikini is regarded as suitable for the beach but not the ballroom, although recent fashion phenomena such as topless dresses and hotpants have had an effect upon this accepted attitude.

Rapid changes in fashion are now commonplace in modern European society where the communications are so influential and fast-operating that a popular film can dictate the current style. In other societies movement in fashion is generally much slower and standards of elegance are sometimes strictly enforced. In traditional Chinese and Japanese society the concept of a 'total look' was of primary importance to those fashionable women and men who could afford the means to achieve it, and a wealthy lady would spend many hours choosing her gown and accessorizing it correctly. The court ladies of Japan wore elaborate multi-layered costumes and paid much attention to harmony in colors and textures.

In addition to wearing ornamental garments many peoples also decorate their bodies by more direct means. The use of body-paint is a very ancient practice, possibly older than costume itself. Even today certain groups, for instance the Australian Aborigines, paint themselves, marking sacred designs on their bodies on ceremonial occasions. Paint and coloring materials are also used for secular or cosmetic purposes, to enhance attractiveness according to the conventions of a particular society. Congolese girls oil their skin and dust themselves with prized red powdered camwood. Noble ladies of the former Chinese court habitually wore a very heavy face make-up. The Dowager Empress Tzu-Hsi used a face-powder made of ground rice and white lead, and a rouge of rose petals on the cheeks and in the center of the lower lip to simulate the small mouth which was then fashionable. Face-powder was introduced from China 59 to Japan where both men and women wore cosmetics, and both sexes also blackened the teeth. Women traditionally blackened their teeth on their wedding day, but courtesans and geishas also practised the custom.

Many peoples also pay great attention to their hair, and bleach, dye, or dress it in a variety of styles which are often symbolic of age or status, but also serve to embellish that most significant part of the body, the head. In traditional Fijian society the men were very hair-conscious, in contrast to their womenfolk, and Fijian men dyed their hair red and yellow with lime and mangrove sap and allowed it to grow into frizzy mops up to four feet across, clipping and training it into fantastic shapes. Hairdressing was regarded as a task for the specialist and important chiefs would spend many hours prior to a ceremony in the hands of their barbers. It is said that one king of Fiji, before making a visit to a neighboring ruler, sat up all night rather than endanger his coiffure. Among some east African tribes such as the Masai and Turkana, men dress their hair with a mixture of grease, clay, and red ocher, and Turkana men can actually carry small articles in their enormous mud-stiffened chignons.

Ornate coiffures were favored in Tibet and Mongolia. Some Tibetan women stiffened their hair with butter and plaited it into numerous braids which fell below the waist. This heavy mantle was supplemented by false hair if necessary, and decorated with many ornaments. The women of central Tibet and the Khalka Mongols dressed their hair with a thick pomade and shaped it into two large flat horns terminating in braids. This coiffure, with its obvious resemblance to cattle horns, had symbolic associations with their pastoral way of life.

Attitudes towards beauty vary according to the conventions of the society concerned. Some practices, involving considerable discomfort and even permanent mutilation, may seem grotesque to outsiders. Many people indulge in more lasting methods of decorating the skin than by using paint or cosmetics. Marking the skin by tattooing is a widespread custom, particularly in Polynesia. A New Zealand Maori male of high rank traditionally began to be tattooed as a youth, and by late middle age his body was covered, literally from head to toe, with glowing blue patterns. Tattooing techniques vary from one place to another. In Polynesia the skin is punctured by gently tapping a sharp-toothed bone tool with a mallet and then rubbing in a staining material which may be vegetable dye or dog's excrement. Among the Eskimo, women formerly tattooed themselves on their chins and cheeks by drawing a thread coated with soot beneath the skin with a needle.

Among the dark-skinned peoples on whom tattooed designs are not clearly visible, the body is ornamented by scarification. The skin is cut with a knife, and soot or some other irritant is rubbed into the wound so as to raise large welts or scars, often in intricate designs.

Scarification is particularly widespread in the Congo, and each tribal group has its own distinctive patterns.

Serious deformation of the body in order to achieve socially conditioned criteria of beauty usually has to begin in infancy. In Borneo baby girls have their foreheads flattened by special padded wooden apparatus. In other regions such as the New Hebrides, and the north-west coast of North America, the back of the head is flattened, or the whole skull is bound to produce an elongated cone-like shape. China had an ancient tradition of foot-binding to produce the tiny feet regarded as essential for a truly beautiful woman. From an early age girls' feet were crushed and tightly bandaged until they became tiny triangular hooves which fitted into embroidered shoes three to four inches long. Chinese literature praised bound feet with precious euphemisms – Golden Lotus, Jade Bamboo Shoots, Twin Wild Ducks – and a considerable body of literature reveals the erotic delights associated with bound feet.

Among the Padaung women of Burma a long giraffe-like neck is regarded as beautiful and in order to achieve this girls wear tightly fitting brass rings about their necks which are gradually increased in number forcing the neck to extend. This practice not only impedes movement and vision but the consequences of removing the rings is positively lethal because the weakened vertebrae collapse.

The insertion of pins and plugs into parts of the face can also produce distortion. South American Indians, Australian Aborigines and many Pacific peoples insert bones through the septum of the nose. The east African Kikuyu admire greatly distended earlobes in women, and girls gradually increase the size of their earplugs until the lobes touch the shoulders or can meet over the crown of the head. Western Eskimo men wear pairs of stone or bone plugs at the lower corners of their mouths, and lip plugs, or labrets, are regarded as essential adjuncts of feminine beauty among the tribes of the north-west coast of North America and in parts of Africa. The Sara women of Lake Chad have their lips pierced on betrothal by their future husbands and pegs are inserted which are steadily increased in size until large discs are worn.

Certain peoples, for instance Australian Aborigines and some Congo tribes, knock out or extract teeth, and others, such as the Malay, inlay their teeth with brass wire and semi-precious stones. All societies – not least our own where ear-piercing, nose operations and face and breast uplifts are undertaken for purely cosmetic reasons – indulge in various practices to shape or mold the body to conform to accepted standards of beauty.

As well as shaping and molding various parts of the anatomy itself, most people also manufacture ornaments with which to adorn the body. The use of ornament is also a very ancient tradition, probably beginning with protective charms; and its function is often more complex than simple decoration. Sometimes ornament may represent a girl's dowry and is worn to attract possible

A Nuba woman's status is indicated by body decorations. Mud is rubbed into knife incisions to produce the desired lace-like scars.

suitors, and frequently it is worn by women as much to impress their own sex as to attract men.

Depending upon the nature of the environment, man exploits every possible material for ornamental purposes: shells, flowers, seeds, teeth, tusks, bone, fur, human hair, feathers, beetle wing-cases, wood, glass, metals and precious and semi-precious stones, while in western society plastics and other synthetic materials are now becoming popular. The desire of different peoples for rare decorative materials which are not available in their own environment has been an important factor in the development of world trade. The jade which was so highly prized and so exquisitely worked by the Chinese had to be quarried thousands of miles away in central Asia, and the precious blue lapis lazuli, coveted in the middle-east and the orient for centuries, originated in Afghanistan.

Costume has always depended on the development of supporting crafts and industries. Probably the earliest resource exploited by man for clothing was the skin of an animal. But even this simple garment required considerable processing before it could be worn because an untreated hide becomes stiff and uncomfortable once it has dried. Many North American Indian tribes wore garments made of deerskin which had been dressed by scraping away the fat and tissue and softening the skin by rubbing in animal fat or brains. But the effect of this treatment is not permanent and usually only lasts as long as the garment is regularly worn. The most permanent method of treating leather is tanning. This involves soaking the skins in a solution of tannic acid and is practised in many parts of the world, particularly in Persia and Turkey. The Eskimo and some Siberian groups evolved tailored fur clothing so finely adapted to their environment that western explorers of the Arctic have had to adopt similar dress in order to survive in it. Eskimo costume is tailored on established patterns and stitched with sinew thread. The furs they use are chiefly seal and caribou – the latter being particularly favored because the hairs are hollow and therefore more effectively trap and retain body heat. Even fish skin has been used for clothing, by the primitive Ainu of north Japan, and the Siberian Gilyak.

As well as furs and skins animal hair in central Asia is made into felt for clothing by alternately beating together and soaking horsehair and wool fibers. A similar technique is used in many parts of the world to produce barkcloth, which is made by beating and soaking the inner bark of suitable trees such as the paper mulberry. The finest barkcloth comes from Polynesia, but it is also manufactured in Indonesia, and in parts of Africa and South America. The grass skirts worn in certain areas of the Pacific are examples of simple clothing made of unprocessed vegetable fibers. Vegetable fibers are also woven into textiles. The Ainu, for instance, formerly made a woven fabric from elmbark, and the north-west coast tribes of North America combined cedarbark fibers with mountain goats' wool for their capes and blankets.

The most suitable fibers for woven textiles are of course wool, silk and cotton. Wool is used in many parts of the world. As well as from the various types of domesticated sheep it is taken from the wild mountain goat in the north-west coast of North America and in Nepal, and from the three kinds of Andean camel (llama, alpaca and vicuna) in Peru. Cotton, both wild and cultivated, grows in India, Africa, South America and the middle east. The arts of silk culture and silk weaving originated centuries ago in China and spread from there to Japan where the silk industry became famous for its gorgeous dyed textiles. Silk fabrics were much prized in the west, and China already plied a lucrative trade along the Silk Route through central Asia long before Roman times.

Man fundamentally clothes himself for protection from an unfavorable environment. His ability to create for himself a portable environment in the form of costume has enabled him to live almost anywhere upon the surface of this planet. Costume, however, serves a multitude of purposes, many of which are socially determined, and the peoples of the world have evolved a fascinating variety of costume and decoration to meet these needs. 61

(Over page) Bejeweled, painted and crowned with eagle plumage, this girl is extremely attractive to the men of New Guinea.

# Man attired

In Omdurman, in Sudan, a member of the Ma'adi family stands outside his family tomb wearing the *jellaba* and turban typical of the Arab world. The snowy whiteness of the garments and shiny newness of his white shoes indicate his affluence.

These spectacular beauty marks, the results of careful and painful scarring, proclaim this woman's membership in the Gobir tribe of the Niger.

In the village of Wakilutad in the Zagros Mountains of Iran a Basseri woman proudly shows off her daughters and her finery.

Uzbek women are skilled at spinning wool and silk, embroidery, weaving, tailoring and felt-making. This child's embroidered woolen cap is typical of northern Afghanistan.

The masked dancer represents a mythical bird in a mystery play performed during the annual *Paro Tse-Chu* lamaist festival held in Bhutan. With the help of the drummer the dancer expels all evil forces after the judgement delivered the King of the Dead.

The Turkomen of sou west Asia usually wea high fleece caps and long, fur-lined coats. Men and women wea the *khala'at*, a brightl colored light gown fc warmer weather. This is often brilliantly embroidered by the women who are also renowned for their manufacture of Bokhara rugs.

## Southern Asia

Among the Padaung of Burma it is considered sexually attractive to have long, giraffe-like necks. Girls wear brass spirals which look like many brass rings and allegedly have the additional desirable property of warding off wild tigers. ·

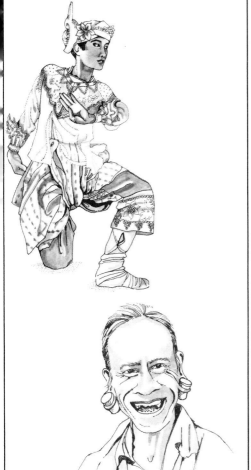

Traditional dancing is a fine art in Thailand, and male dancers are as common as female ones. The costumes and headdresses are designed according to the tale or legend on which the dance is based.

Y Bang Bu Prek is a Vietnamese village sorcerer. He conducts the rituals necessary to ensure the help of the good spirits and control the evil ones. He wears large ivory plugs in his earlobes and has paid a local 'dentist' one chicken for filing down four of his teeth.

## Western-dominated world

A Dutch woman takes some time off from her meticulous housekeeping. She is wearing the traditional costume of the Netherlands with the famous wooden shoes, but is without the typical Dutch white winged cap on her flaxen plaits.

In the mountains of Greece an old grandmother finds both pleasure and profit in making sweaters for sale. The wool is shorn from the family's sheep and goats, soaked in the sea, bleached, dyed and spun at home.

Wigs have been worn throughout history for different purposes and with various meanings. Sumerians, Egyptians and the ancient Greeks and Romans used them to simulate real hair. Only in the 17th century did Louis XIII start the fashion for wigs like this one, today worn in England only by judges and barristers in law-courts.

# Man attired

Black Africa

Australasia

This woman in south-west Africa is wearing an elaborate Ekori ceremonial headdress.

A man in Arnhemland Australia, is undergoing a secret ceremony to lift a taboo. His body is first washed and shaved, then painted in totemic patterns with earth colors mixed with orchid juice.

When a Sara woman of Chad becomes betrothed, her lips are pierced by her intended husband who inserts a peg into the incision. Gradually the peg is changed for a larger one and finally large discs are worn.

The *kondo-chindu* headdress of this New Guinea tribesman is made of human hair supplemented by feathers and other brightly colored fiber.

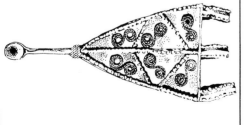

People of central Asia use ornately carved utensils like this for removing the wax from their ears.

The Aborigines of Australia paint ceremonial designs on each other's back. As they go half naked in the heat of the day, the decorations can be appreciated by all.

## Amerindia

## Orient

The Waura Indians of Brazil are elaborately made up for their war games. They are painted from top to toe in designs both geometric and animal; the colors are mainly black, white and red.

This Eskimo woman from east Greenland wears the traditional costume of furs and skins which she sews with sinew thread. These clothes are only worn out of doors: at night inside the house adults and children strip down to a leather G-string.

The Akha grow rice in the hills of northern Laos and neighboring Burma, Thailand and China. They live in villages at elevations of 4,000 feet, and their women are distinguished by their elaborate headdresses and jewelry.

On the Chinese mainland 'people's opera' has replaced the ancient traditional art. In Taiwan opera singers still don the old costumes to play the old roles in operas that have remained unchanged for centuries.

Eskimo travel the vast polar snow lands with their dog packs. They invariably wear the fur parkas, mittens and hoods which they are practically born into.

The Atayal tribe of aborigines in Taiwan live in secluded mountain villages and special permits are required to visit them. They extract their back teeth believing this enhances their beauty. They also tattoo their foreheads, but only headhunters may tattoo their chins and only women who are skillful weavers may tattoo their cheeks.

# Man attired

Berber women from Middle Atlas villages are freer than their Arab sisters in the towns. Most of them do not wear the veil, and they are free to tattoo their faces and paint their hair and hands with henna.

Many women in the Muslim world have already been liberated from the veil, mainly in rural areas where their husbands' need for their help in the fields overcomes their desire to keep them secluded. But in many towns the veil still prevails, often decorated with as many heavy coins as its wearer can carry.

The Amhara of Ethiopia have been Christians since the reign of King Ezana of Axum during the 4th century AD. Their priests are held in high esteem and wear stunning clothes liberally decorated with gold thread. Their crosses are equally splendid both in design and execution.

## Central and northern Asia

The Udege people of Siberia have earned themselves a reputation for their fine embroidery. When Chinese cotton replaced fish skins in the late 19th century they made the most of the new material and their national dress is rich and colorful.

At a wedding in the Lahul valley, in the Kashmir-India border region, the bride wears the traditional white shawl of hand woven wool. The headdress, handed down from mother to daughter, is studded with rough turquoise stones, alleged to be protective. The heavy silver rings, locally made and carved are a status symbol, indicative of the family's wealth.

Jovni Kitti is 70 years old. Short and strong, this wiry Lapp has been toughened by his long and arduous life. He is wearing the richly embroidered national dress, with the distinctive Lapp ribboned hat.

## Southern Asia

One of the great fascinations of the far east is the beauty and mystery of the women, who are brought up to serve men and strive to please them.

A devout Hindu pilgrim to the temple of the goddess Ganga has the word 'Rama' written in Hindi all over her face and sari. This indicates her devotion to that god who is the symbol of the ideal man.

Members of tribes from all over India come to New Delhi for the annual Republic Day Parade. Dressed up for the occasion, the men and women come with all their best jewelry: earrings, noserings, and lip- and cheek-plugs.

## Western-dominated world

Involved in fierce combat at the Highland Games, these two Scots can easily be identified with their clans by the colors and patterns of the tartan kilts they wear.

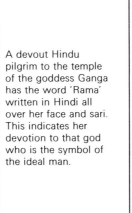

In predominantly Roman Catholic Sicily, this woman stands out as a member of the Greek Orthodox enclave in Piana degli Albanesi. Her traditional clothes are family heirlooms, handed from mother to daughter for many generations.

*Haute couture* is said to be dying out, and is increasingly replaced by ready-made off-the-peg fashions. But many women still buy their bridal gowns at expensive salons, and many would love to be married in this creation from the Paris house of Nina Ricci.

# Man attired

## Black Africa

Young women of the nomadic Bororo tribe of Niger wear long brass anklets which they polish to a gleaming golden finish with sand and mud. They stop wearing them after the birth of their second child.

This young woman from Mopti, on the Niger river, may well be wearing her dowry in her ears: two enormous hunks of gold, set where she can take good care of them at all times.

Women of the Ndebele tribe in southern Africa spend their time making bead jewelry which they sell to tourists. They themselves wear large bead bracelets, necklets and anklets and their homes are cheerfully decorated in geometric patterns.

## Australasia

Concepts of decency and modesty vary enormously: this New Guinea tribesman exposes his testicles, but his penis is encased in a gourd sheath, and it is considered immodest to remove it in public.

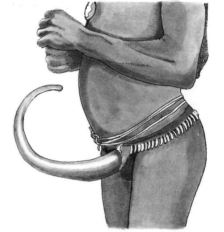

In the central highlands of New Guinea, Chimbu tribesmen parade in ceremonial dress. They wear parrot feathers and bird-of-paradise plumes in their headdresses, more feathers and shell discs in their noses. Boar tusks hang around their necks and shells around their waists. The traditional drum is hour-glass shaped.

This Bena Bena tribesman from the eastern highlands of New Guinea is wearing a ceremonial mask and headdress. The feathers come from a cassowary bird and the boar tusks on his wooden mask are a status symbol among his cannibalistic Goroka people.

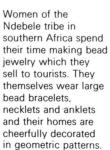

## Amerindia

This decorative comb, found among the Indians of Alaska, is carved and inlaid with abalone shell. The design portrays Chief Shaikes and his guardian spirit.

This Seri Indian girl has her face painted in the way traditional to her nation. The paints are made from special colored rocks ground to powder.

Among the Waura of Brazil it is customary for men to don straw suits and woven masks and come into the kitchen demanding food. The game includes threats uttered in falsetto voices and menacing fish-toothed weapons. The masks represent dangerous water spirits as described by men who had been sick and were saved by the shaman.

## Orient

This Japanese peasant woman has to hold up her kimono while working in the rice fields. Her *obi* (sash) is no more functional. But the large round hat is perfectly suited to long hours spent under a hot sun.

The Japanese geisha is always elegantly dressed and meticulously groomed. She can be identified as a geisha by the special pattern of her *obi* and her kimono.

An Ainu chief from the village of Shiraoi in northern Japan wears full tribal dress; the long beards of the Ainu, the 'hairy' people, distinguish them from other Japanese.

71

# Man the music-maker

In many traditional societies music is so much a part of life that little or no activity can be imagined without it. This is not, of course, true in our western European culture, where we must make a separate 'study' of music if we are to understand it. We tend, therefore, to forget that in the greater part of the world hunting and fishing, planting and sowing, house-building and tent moving, boat building and launching, paddling and walking, milling and threshing, hauling water from deep wells or mining rock salt in the desert, birth and death, circumcision and marriage, illness and its cure, theater and dancing, entertainment and passing on of news, family history and genealogy, as well as all forms of worship, are inconceivable without music.

Of music in the stone age we can never know anything definite. We do, however, know that music existed even in paleolithic times, for bone flutes, jingles, scrapers and bullroarers have been excavated. In neolithic times instruments included clay drums, shell trumpets, and lithophones. When we consider that only instruments made of the most durable material (bone or stone, later clay or metal), or that instruments embedded in sand, ice or peat deposits were likely to be preserved, while those of wood, bamboo or leather would perish, we begin to have some idea of the prevalence of music in paleolithic and neolithic times.

Rhythm is basic not only to music but to all bodily movements. A great many instruments exist mainly to emphasize rhythm. Just as simple hand-clapping may accompany singing and dancing, two pieces of wood may be clapped together instead. Such clappers are known in antiquity: the Egyptians produced wood or ivory ones in the form of hands clapping, and simple wooden concussion sticks are still used by Australian aborigines. The Aderi of the Ethiopian city of Harar used them during Muslim religious ceremonies; they provide the basic percussion for Chinese and Vietnamese classical music; Spanish castanets are well-known instruments of this type. Cymbals too are clappers made of metal.

An alternative to clapping hands is stamping feet. Stamping feet has led to stamping tubes, usually of bamboo, either on the ground or against another piece of bamboo or wood. Aboriginal tribes of the Malay jungles use stamping tubes today to accompany group singing and dancing. In Java and Bali these are part of their highly developed music.

Man's ingenuity in devising ways of marking or emphasizing rhythm is immense. From the huge slit-drums of Fiji or New Guinea to the small formalized fish-shaped versions which are used in Buddhist ceremonies; from the so-called rock-gongs of west Africa, where the resonant stone remains in the ground – the list could extend almost endlessly.

Scrapers (rasps or notched sticks) existed in paleolithic times, when they were made of bone, and are one of the very oldest forms of rhythm producers. They were considered to have had magical powers: kill an animal, make a scraper of its bone, use this instrument in the pre-hunt ritual, and you ensure success in the coming hunt. In modern times we find washboards and gourd scrapers (South American tribal instruments) in our dance bands.

So far we have only spoken of rhythmical devices without specific pitch. Many percussion instruments, however, are precisely tuned, and thus provide melody as well as rhythm. Lithophones or stone chimes are a basic of Chinese and Vietnamese music. Xylophones are found in most of Africa south of the Sahara, often in elaborate orchestras, or as accompaniment for flutes, horns or drums. Similarly, a whole series of instruments, often as many as twenty, made of tuned metal bars and tuned gongs, comprise the gamelan orchestras of Java and Bali.

One thing which the materials of which these instruments are made have in common is resonance. A bronze gong is beaten, a notched bone is scraped, a xylophone is struck, a rattle is shaken. It is the material which is resonant and responds to being struck. These instruments are all called idiophones, or self-sounding instruments. In Africa the *sansa* has flexible iron tongues fixed to a resonator, and the vibrating length of these tongues can easily be adjusted. The *sansa* is found all over Africa south of the Sahara; it can be made of whatever materials are locally available – the iron tongues are often flattened bicycle or umbrella spokes, and the resonator is a box, a gourd, a metal cooking pot or even a tin can. It is as simple to play as it is cheap, and easy to make and carry. And its music is so sweet and pleasant that one can understand why so many love songs are played on it.

Another idiophone belonging to this melodic group is the jews harp (or mouth-harp). In South-east Asia jews harps are made of bamboo or sugar palm. In Europe and the middle east they are of iron. They are held so that the tongue of the instrument vibrates between the player's teeth, and a tune is played by changing the shape of the mouth cavity. The tone is so delicate that the instrument tends to accompany love songs – indeed, in several areas, its music is considered so seductive that it is forbidden to play it during planting and harvest time.

The most common instrument associated with rhythm and percussion is the drum. All drums have one characteristic in common – the sound is produced by vibrating a membrane stretched over a frame. Drums belong to the second class of musical instruments, membranophones.

Drums are most frequently made of wood, although metal, pottery and gourd are also common materials. Some have a single skin, some double. Some have rattles or scrapers added. Drums may be tiny or huge. They may be easy to carry or so heavy that they have to be dragged, with difficulty, to where they are played. Most tribes possess some form of drum. The few which do not may use the services of a drum and player from a neighboring tribe, or they may make a temporary drum by covering the mouth of a water jar, for example, with a

In a village in the
Peruvian highlands a
*mariachi* band sends a gay,
brassy tune through
the thin clear air.

In a village in the
Peruvian highlands a
*mariachi* band sends a gay,
brassy tune through
the thin clear air.

skin which they bang on. It would appear that drums existed during the neolithic period and the great civilizations of antiquity, Mesopotamia, Babylon, Egypt, India, Greece and Rome, all show representations of drums in paintings, carvings or statuettes. Some of the actual instruments still exist.

Possibly because of their great antiquity drums are associated with ritual, magic and legend. In some parts of west Africa every part of drum making is accompanied by sacrifice and prayer, while some east African tribesmen make daily offerings to the drums. They are so sacred that even a criminal is safe if he reaches the sanctuary of the drumyard. In all the major religions of the world – Islam, Judaism, early Christianity, and Buddhism, as well as animism – the drum has been, or still is, used as an indispensable part of worship. Finally, drums were used to frighten the enemy in war, and to encourage one's own soldiers to advance. This applies not only to tribal societies in Africa and Asia but also to Europe from medieval times until the beginning of the 20th century.

Drums may be tubular (cylindrical, barrel-shaped, conical, hour-glass, footed, goblet-shaped, or handle drums); or they may be kettledrums, with a pot or vessel forming the body; or they may be frame drums, which have a narrow frame instead of a body upon which to stretch the membrane. Tubular drums, which can have one or two heads, have by far the greatest variety of shapes and sizes and include the *tabla* of classical Indian music, with its effective tuning-chok system and the Arabic *darabuka* which accompanies both folk and classical music. One very interesting tubular drum is the 'talking drum' of West Africa. This is hour-glass shaped, with the heads connected by hide lacings, so that pressure of the player's arm on the central portion of the drum changes the tension of the skin, and produces low, higher or high notes. In the areas of west Africa which have tonal languages, it is thus possible to play the melodic pattern of a word. The drums can be heard for miles, and messages transmitted in drum language.

The instruments with which most people are familiar – indeed, what they tend to mean by musical instruments – are melody instruments, either wind instruments, aerophones, or stringed instruments, cordophones.

Aerophones – except for the bullroarer which is whirled by many primitive peoples – are blown and are basically of three types: flutes, reed instruments, and horns and trumpets. Bone flutes, evidence of prehistoric man's interest in melody, are found in paleolithic sites. In the high civilizations of antiquity, and in widely separated parts of the world all the types of wind instruments which we know today were played.

Flutes are sounded by the player blowing obliquely across the sharp edge of a mouth-hole. The simplest flute is merely a bamboo tube with a sharpened edge. This is, however, very difficult to play, although Arabs and Berber of the Sahara play one, as do some tribes of South-east Asia, and the kaval of the Balkans belongs to this type. The more common form of this end-blown flute is a compound instrument, the pan-pipes, or syrinx. Here a series of small end-blown flutes of different lengths, without fingerholes, but stopped at the base, are bound together: each tube gives one note. Pan-pipes are found in such disparate areas as pre-Columbian South America, ancient China, Greece and Rome.

Perhaps the oldest form of flute, found in paleolithic times, is the more complicated duct flute, in which the upper end is blocked off, except for a small duct which directs the player's breath against a sharp edge cut in the tube below. The simplest forms have external ducts, as in Indonesia, but they may also have a mouthpiece as in the European recorder – or any gradation between. Duct flutes, like notched flutes, are found on every continent; they are extremely easy to play well. Often players have developed formalized ensembles with a set traditional repertoire of very beautiful music. Many duct flutes are globular such as whistles, ocarinas, and bird-calls. Again, these pottery whistles are fairly old, and in one area, South and Central America, thousands of examples have been discovered, many of them more than a thousand years old.

A final, and later, form of flute, the transverse or cross flute, has the upper end blocked, and a mouth-hole cut into the side of the tube, which is held horizontally. From the simple silver-bronze flutes of ancient Peru, with only two fingerholes, and the simple bamboo flutes of China (which nevertheless play the great classical music of the far east) they have developed into the complex orchestral instrument of the European classical music.

Reed instruments may have a single beating reed (clarinet), a double beating reed (oboe) or a freely vibrating reed (for example the mouth organ). The beating reed instruments have a somewhat hard, shrill tone and the free reed instruments a soft and delicate one. All are known in the great ancient eastern civilizations and may 73

Introduced during British
rule, the brass band is now
very popular in India. This one
leads the parade at the fall
festival of Duvali in Delhi.

in fact be much older.

Simple clarinets usually have a reed cut into the sides of a piece of cane, and this reed is inserted into a cylinder with fingerholes; they occur most frequently in pairs as in the Arabic *zummara*. The reed of the western European clarinet is bound against the edge of an opening and there is a system of keys which permits a chromatic scale and a compass of several octaves – but this part of our orchestra is basically an 18th century invention. Simple clarinet reeds are still in use in bagpipes of the Arabic world and the Greek islands, as well as in the drone pipes of most other European bagpipes.

In the double reed instruments, or oboes, the two reeds, bound together onto a staple, beat against each other and are inserted into the upper end of a tube with fingerholes, which generally widens at the base. Well known in antiquity, this type of instrument exists today in the Muslim world, where it is called *algaita* or *gaita*, in India and South-east Asia where it is called *surnai*; it is also prevalent throughout the far east, where it is used both in Buddhist ceremonies and in classical music performances. Double reed instruments came to Europe from the east and these folk shawms – which later changed into the oboe we know today – have been an important part of our music since the Middle Ages.

One of the most complicated of all instruments is the organ. Blowing to sound an organ was mechanized nearly two thousand years ago by the Greeks and Romans and developed from the early Greek 'water organs' to the small bellow-blown organ of Byzantium, to Spain in the 5th century, England in the 8th century, and Europe generally in the 10th century. The churches had large and loud organs, but portative organs were used for secular music from the 12th century.

Horns and trumpets, the third major group of aerophones, use the compressed lips of the player as a device for sounding the instrument, just as the sharpened edge interrupts the flow of air into a flute. In general horns are more or less conical in bore, and trumpets cylindrical, but with the folk instruments the sharp differentiation does not often exist. There are a great many variations in shape and form, from the side-blown wooden trumpets of the Pacific Islands to the ivory horns – end or side-blown – of Africa; from the conch-shell trumpets of India, Spain or Oceania to the long straight metal trumpets of Central Asia, Tibet, and the Arabic world, as well as Europe.

The most familiar instruments, to western Europeans, are the stringed instruments, or cordophones. Most of us could name any number of them – violin, 'cello, double bass, guitar, harp, piano, lute, harpsichord, banjo, dulcimer, psaltery, zither, mandolin – to say nothing of the Indian sitar. These instruments can all be subdivided into four main classes: musical bows and harps; lyres; lutes and fiddles and zithers. As many areas of the world have no stringed instruments, cordophones may be the

Introduced during British rule, the brass band is now very popular in India. This one leads the parade at the fall festival of Duvali in Delhi.

newcomers on the musical scene. Their origins are sometimes ascribed to the hunter's bow.

The high civilizations of the near east gave birth to most of the stringed instruments whose descendants are played today. But the simpler societies began with simple musical bows. The string is under tension and when it is pushed against the shoulder the note is lower. These simple musical bows, tapped with a small stick, give very little sound, so a resonator, usually a gourd, was added. Sometimes the string was divided into two unequal parts and two notes could thus be obtained. Holding the resonator against the player's body, or the end of the bow in the player's mouth gave additional volume. Rock carvings in southern Africa show several of these instruments played in concert, It seems probable that the multiple musical bow or pluriarc (which puts several differently sized bows onto one resonator) developed from this use of the musical bow. From there it is a small step to bow-harps which are still prevalent in many parts of Africa. But the angle harp, strengthened in the corner, could take strings of greater tension, and thus the eastern harps became quite elaborate. In Europe the final development of the harp took place: a column was added to strengthen the body of the instrument. In medieval times the Celtic harp had a curved column. Later this was changed into the more familiar straight column.

The great stringed instrument of antiquity, however, was not the harp, but the lyre. This instrument consists of a resonator and two arms protruding from it; these are connected by a cross bar, to which the strings are fastened. Only as many notes are obtainable as there are strings. There were two major forms of the instrument – a rectangular body with asymmetrical arms, and a lighter and more portable type with round body and symmetrical arms. Both existed in Mesopotamia, Israel (the 'harp' of David was a lyre), Greece and Rome.

Most familiar perhaps are the instruments of the third class of cordophones – lutes and fiddles. These instruments have a body and neck, which permits the vibrating length of the strings – and thus the pitch – to be changed by stopping them with the fingers. Lutes are plucked, fiddles are bowed. In form they vary a great deal, more, indeed, than any other type of instrument. Some fiddles are carved of one piece of wood, such as the Greek *lyra* or the Arabic *rebab* (our viols and violins are a development from this type of instrument). There are also the globular-bodied fiddles of Baluchistan or the Indian *sarinda*, all of which are bowed. Lutes, on the other hand, may have either a short neck and large body, such as the *el'ud* of the Arabic world (which gives us our English word 'lute') or the *p'ip'a* of China. Others have a long thin neck and small body. The nomadic tribes often use this type of lute, which is easy to carry and also less prone to damage. One special form, the spike fiddle, of the Muslim world, is bowed. Its neck pierces its body and rests either on the ground or on the player's knee. The West African *kora* has a large gourd resonator, covered with skin, and the long neck goes through the gourd. The bridge of the *kora*, however, is at right-angles to the face of the resonator and, when the two dozen or so strings are in place, the instrument becomes as much a harp as a lute.

Finally, we come to the fourth major class of cordophones: zithers. These have strings stretched over bridges, either separate or incorporated in the body; the strings stretch across the entire instrument and parallel to it. A resonator may be added but, more commonly, the entire instrument acts as a resonator. The strings may be plucked, but some are struck with beaters, in which case the instrument is called a dulcimer.

A simple type of zither is a bar with raised frets and a gourd resonator at each end. The north Indian *vina* was of this type, although today the form has changed. There are tube zithers in South-east Asia and Madagascar; trough zithers in east and central Africa. The great majority, however, are board (or box) zithers. It is from forms such as the *qanun* (from Turkey) that our plucked keyboard instruments – virginals, spinets and harpsichords – derive. The struck dulcimers, such as the *santur* or the Hungarian *cembalom*, resulted in the development of the clavichord and pianoforte.

Broadly speaking, there are two types of music, although the line which divides them is not sharp and clearly defined. Ethnic music consists basically of traditional material, orally transmitted. The ethnic group may be neolithic man in England, a non-literate group in Africa, a literate group in the Balkans or western Europe, but this traditional (or folk) music plays a definite and important part in the culture of the entire group. Art music, on the other hand, is a convenient term for both classical and liturgical music; it is consciously and usually theoretically defined, and is generally in written form. Ethnic music is sometimes performed by professional musicians; art music is almost entirely so. Since there are systems of classical music in the far east, Indonesia, India, Persia and the Arab world as well as Europe and the Americas, it is obvious that ethnic and art music often exist side by side. In an era of transistor radios, commercial popular music also exists alongside both, sometimes changing or even ousting the traditional folk music. Each type of music – ethnic, classical, and liturgical – contributes to, and borrows from, the others.

All the classical systems of music – the Indian *raga*, Arabic *maqam*, Chinese, Indonesian and European – are based upon a division of the octave into notes to which the instruments are tuned. These instruments are precisely tuned – to a lithophone in China, to a metallophone in the gamelan orchestra of Java or a tuning fork in Europe. Or they may be tuned to a relative pitch within the octave.

While the earliest social or religious demands were for instruments to emphasize rhythm, pitch has been important for many thousands of years. When several instruments were played together, the concept of pitch became extremely important, and devices were necessary for keeping instruments in tune, not only with themselves but with others. With this development (and some peoples have not yet reached that stage) new means of keeping instruments in tune proliferated. Tuning rings or pegs, and movable bridges, appeared on stringed instruments, tuning chocs or lacings in drums, interchangeable parts or sets of instruments were used on aerophones. New types of reeds and of strings appeared; instruments which could not meet the greater needs of a new period dropped out, to be replaced by new instruments which in turn made more demands on the older instruments. Composers kept pace, or even accelerated, the rate of change. The orchestras depicted on Egyptian tombs, like those of Tibetan monasteries, or central Asian courts, or European opera houses, all have in common the need to produce music to fit the needs of the group. Craftsmen invented and built instruments; artists composed for and played upon these instruments. Together they made the music which society desired or demanded.

75

(Over page) Each followed by his own drummer, Aṣhanti chiefs in Ghana gather to mourn the old king and celebrate the election of the new.

# Man the music-maker

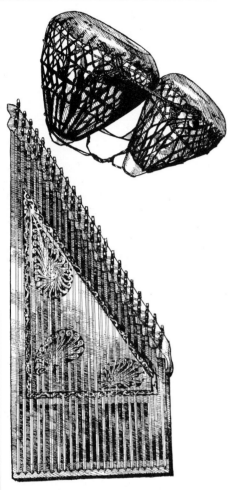

A double kettledrum from Morocco made of pottery covered with hide. It is 44 cm high. This instrument, called a *naqara* in Arabic, was introduced to Europe during the Crusades. In England these easily carried drums became known as nakers.

A *qanun* from Turkey, 93 cm high. The *qanun* has hardly changed since the 10th century when it was introduced to Europe via north Africa and Spain.

The strange wailing sound characteristic of north African Arab music is produced by this horn, played in Djemna, Tunisia.

The *rebab*, being played here by a boy in Baluchistan, is a member of the bowed lute family.

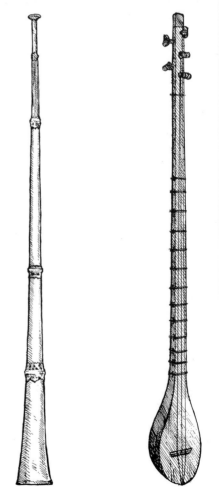

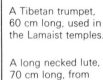

A Tibetan trumpet, 60 cm long, used in the Lamaist temples.

A long necked lute, 70 cm long, from central Asia.

## Southern Asia

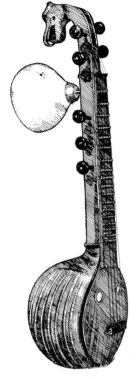

A *vina* from south India, 125 cm long. The *vina* is a classical instrument which has developed from the zither into a long lute with an extra resonator.

A Meo tribesman from northern Thailand plays a traditional bamboo mouth organ.

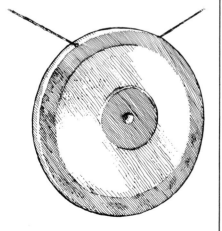

A gong from Borneo, 60 cm across. Gongs originated in Asia, probably in the mountainous country between Tibet and Burma.

## Western-dominated world

A harpsichord keyboard, 75 cm long. The harpsichord is not, as would at first appear, related to the piano. It is a development of the plucked zither.

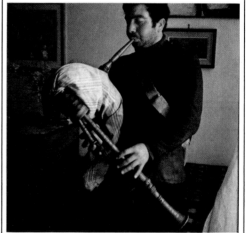

Italian bagpipes. Bagpipes are ancient and complex reed instruments. Their origins cannot be traced exactly but they existed in ancient Persia, Egypt, Chaldea and Greece.

The violin is one of the great classical and folk instruments of the world.

The clarinet illustrated on the left was made in Brussels in the 1840s. It is 66 cm long. In its simplest form this reed instrument is made by small boys all over Europe from a reed or cornstalk. Unlike most other instruments, which have long and complicated histories, the clarinet was invented by J C Denner, a recorder maker from Nuremburg who died in 1707. The mouthpiece with the reed is separate.

79

# Man the music-maker

A talking drum from Nigeria, 58 cm long. Pressure on the lacing at the waist will tighten the membrane and raise the note. The player uses the drum's ability to change notes to reproduce the tones of the Yoruba language.

This wooden carving, 45 cm high, shows how the talking drums are played.

A side-blown ivory horn from Nigeria. It is 33 cm long. This one is made from the tusk of an elephant.

A line of dancing men in the central highland of New Guinea beat time with bamboo stamping tubes.

A carved wooden *nguru*, a whistle made by the Maori of New Zealand. It is 17 cm long.

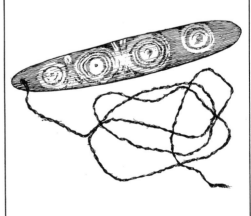

A bullroarer, 29 cm long, from Australia. Bullroarers have been found in paleolithic sites. They act direct on the air, producing whirring noise as the are whirled round. The instrument plays an important part in the ritual of many tribes. some aboriginal tribe it is used in initiation ceremonies and is so sacred that women, children and the uninitiated may not see or even hear it.

## Amerindia

## Orient

Panpipes are ancient instruments found in many parts of the world. They may be made of wood or pottery, or in this case, cane. The player is a headman of the Tukano Indians of the Piraparaná river in Colombia.

Bronze cymbals from China, 21 cm in diameter.

Most whistles have at least one finger hole, but this shell shaped whistle from Chiclayo, Peru, has none. It dates from 1100 AD and is 18 cm long.

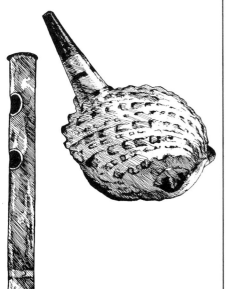

A group playing the long, fretted Korean zither.

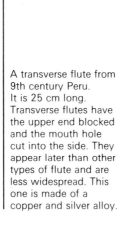

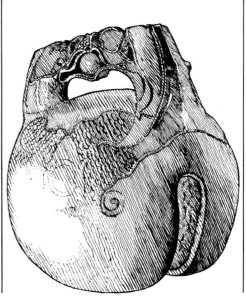

A transverse flute from 9th century Peru. It is 25 cm long. Transverse flutes have the upper end blocked and the mouth hole cut into the side. They appear later than other types of flute and are less widespread. This one is made of a copper and silver alloy.

A wooden *mu yii* or 'fish' from China, 24 cm high. The fish is stylized, lacquered in red and gold and carved out of camphor wood. The head and tail come together to form a handle. Beaten with a heavy stick it summons divine attention and is considered especially useful in prayers for rain. Large ones are used as temple instruments by both Buddhist and Taoist priests and smaller ones are used by pilgrims.

81

# Man the music-maker

An Arab playing a *rebab*. This one is much more primitive than the one shown on page 78 but even a crude home-made instrument can give as much pleasure as an elegantly finished one.

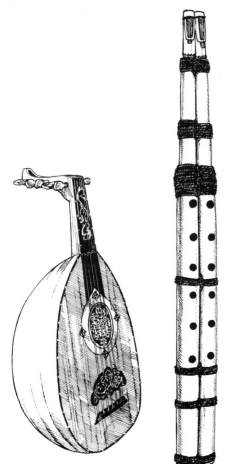

A *zummara* from Tunisia 36 cm long. This instrument is played with the whole of the tongue vibrating reed in the mouth.

A short lute from Syria, 81 cm long. Short lutes have a neck which is shorter than the body. They have spread throughout the far east, middle east and the whole of the Islamic world into Europe.

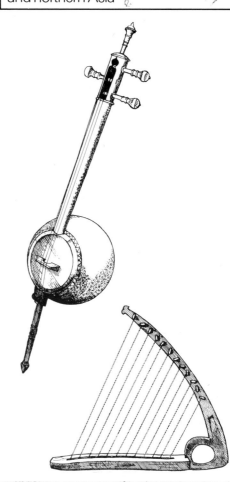

A Persian *kemanje* or three stringed fiddle, 78 cm high.

An 18th century angle harp from the Caucasus mountains, 62 cm high. Angle harps appeared in western Asia and Egypt more than 4,000 years ago. Originating probably in Persia, they spread westward into the Arabic speaking countries and east through central Asia and Turkestan as far as China.

A beautifully painted *morienhur* or two-stringed fiddle from Urga in Mongolia. It is 90 cm high.

## Southern Asia

## Western-dominated world

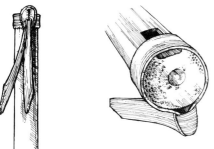

A bamboo duct flute from southern Asia, 50 cm long. Duct flutes have the upper end blocked except for the small duct into which the player blows and which directs the breath to the sharp edge of an opening, cut into the tube. The duct can be internal, as illustrated by the small drawing; or external, terminal or central.

The Music Lesson' by Jan Steen (1626-1679) hangs in the National Gallery in London. All well-brought-up young ladies of the time had to know how to play the harpsichord.

The Indian *tabla* (29 cm high) is tuned by means of the chocks under the lacings.

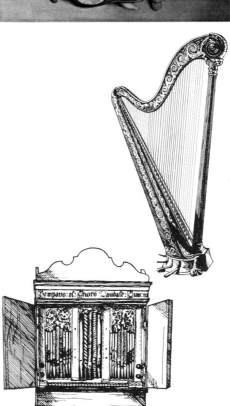

An 18th century frame harp, 185 cm high.

A *gamelan* orchestra in Java. Metallophones are found throughout south-east Asia, reaching their most highly developed form in Indonesia.

A chamber organ from the 17th century (214 cm).

83

# Man the music-maker

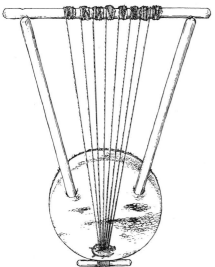

A bowl lyre from Africa (101 cm). These lyres are very common in Africa — in Congo, Gabon, Uganda, Kenya, Tanzania, Ethiopia and southern Sudan. Resonators are generally wooden bowls covered with skin.

Xylophones originated long ago but they are played in a great many areas today. There are two main ways of producing the graduated series of notes. Either the length or the thickness of the bars is varied — the larger or thicker the bar the deeper the note.

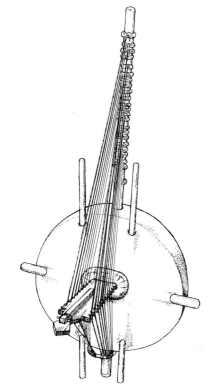

The *kora*, a harp-lute is played by professional musicians in Mali, Guinea and Senegal to accompany singing. It usually has up to 21 strings. The body is covered in cow or male antelope skin and the neck and bridge are made of African rosewood. It is 105 cm high.

The simplest musical instrument of all is just two sticks knocked together by the primitive Aborigines of Australia.

A slit drum made from a hollowed out tree trunk. It comes from the area around the upper course of the Digul river in West Irian. It was the custom to take these drums to the men's house and drop them onto the wooden floor. As it struck the floor the drum made a sound like thunder. At that moment the spirit entered the drum.

A side-blown trumpet from New Guinea, 40 cm long.

## Amerindia

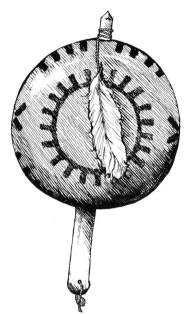

A Hopi Indian rattle from north-east Arizona. It is made from a gourd which is left to dry until the pulp and seeds come loose. Then a hole is made for the handle and the pulp carefully picked out. Rattles are usually decorated with feathers and painted with symbols representing clouds, rain, hail and other elemental and mythological figures.

The drum is an important part of Eskimo life. Songs and dances to the accompaniment of the sealskin drum were held to cement friendships, celebrate a hunt or just to enliven the long Arctic nights.

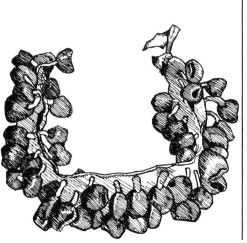

A nut shell dancing belt used by South American Indians. Nut shells are the most common objects used on jingles in both Africa and South America, although cowrie shells and bits of bone are also used. This belt is 25 cm wide.

## Orient

A beautifully carved conch shell trumpet from 18th century India (19 cm long). The conch shell is one of the earliest instruments to appear in India. It is mentioned in the earliest sacred writings as a means of terrifying the enemy in battle. Today it continues to be used as a temple instrument.

The jews harp or mouth harp has a tongue enclosed in a frame of metal, wood or as here, bamboo. The frame is supported by the teeth and the tongue of the harp is plucked while the mouth acts as a resonator.

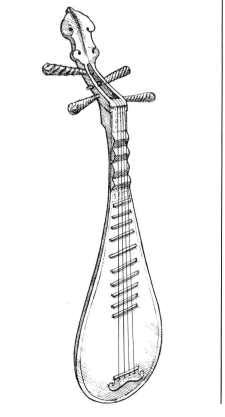

The *p'ip'a*, a short lute, used in China. The silk strings are fastened to a cross bar on the wooden sound board and the frets on the neck are raised. Length: 60 cm.

# Man the traveler

We have today reached the incredible situation in which the tranquil oceanic scene of outrigger dugout canoes sailing on blue seas can be shattered in an instant by the scream of earthshrinking jet airplanes passing overhead. In England, virtually on the writer's doorstep, tourists can arrive in a sun-roofed luxury coach to visit the last of the English coracle makers at Ironbridge in Shropshire. In our modern era of spacecraft and nuclear powered submarines, when the paddle steamer and trolleybus are affectionately remembered as obsolete transport devices, and dirigible airships as positively antideluvian, it is perhaps easy to forget that there still survive in active use much simpler means of 'getting from A to B'. Although pre-industrial man has been stereotyped as a species of narrow, introspective humanity with restricted geographical horizons, the carriage of goods and persons from one place to another is an important activity at all levels of human organization, and it is characterized by a considerable display of ingenuity.

The scale and complexity of transportation among pre-industrial folk is frequently underestimated. Through the millennia there has been constant interaction between human groups involving trade, migration, and conquest – without the aid of the complex devices and machines which are the pride of an industrial age. Peoples in some environments, for example where there is excessive cold or aridity, move themselves and their belongings according to seasonal fluctuations which govern their food supplies – although the influence of climate and other ecological factors has frequently been exaggerated. Even in a hunting and gathering economy such as that of the Tanzanian Hadza, whose degree of control over environmental resources is minimal, their periodic relocations of camp sites and casual wanderings are surprisingly free from the limitations of food and water availability. Incentives for transportation are generally far more complex than those of physical determinants. They are connected with a whole range of economic, social and political interests of individuals and groups.

The Yap Islanders in Micronesia obtained supplies of stone from which they fashioned their unique stone currency from an island many hundreds of miles away. The perilous canoe journey to and from the stone quarries called for superb seamanship and claimed the lives of a large proportion of the sailors, so that the stone retained a high scarcity value. The exploitation of the stone quarries was surrounded by ritual, and the distribution of the different denominations of currency played a vital role in traditional political processes. In the western Pacific there exists a highly organized system of exchange called the *kula* featuring shell valuables. *Kula* expeditions take the 'argonauts' in fleets of canoes for long voyages between the islands of eastern Papua, so that shell necklaces may be exchanged for shell armrings by *kula* partners. Each type of valuable always travels through the islands in the same direction: the necklaces clockwise and the arm-rings anticlockwise. The ceremonial and political aspects of the *kula* far outweigh any direct economic significance.

It is only in their myths and other supernatural beliefs that pre-industrial peoples move through the air. Land and water are the two great realms of primitive transport.

The simplest way to travel is to walk. Often there is no alternative. For walking there have been two main adaptations: there are accessories for walking, and there are carrying devices. Walking aids are most highly developed in snowy and icy regions. Eskimo make great use of snowshoes. Europeans favor skis. In many parts of the world people still go barefoot. In parts of Africa today rubber sandals made from old car and lorry tires are worn. Loads can be carried much more efficiently by using devices which leave the hands relatively free and distribute the weight. Although carrying a load in a knapsack or shopping bag appears 'natural' to the average modern European, there is much cross-cultural variation in the devices and methods used to carry burdens. In black Africa loads are predominantly carried on a head-pad. And some Amerindians prefer the basket with tumpline. Particularly in the mountainous areas of the world, hundreds of miles may be covered on foot by hawkers carrying goods in packs or crates on their backs to outlying markets and homes. The Sherpas who assist in Himalayan expeditions, and lines of porters trudging through the African bush, are figures of great appeal to the popular imagination, though the latter are being superseded by the jeep.

Some carrying devices require the co-operation of two or more people. Examples include the carrying pole by

Perhaps the most versatile beast of burden, the elephant has been used for war, ceremony, and heavy traction work.

which dead animals or war victims are borne in parts of Oceania, and the highly developed sedan chair.

Before the era of mechanical propulsion using domesticated animals and traction devices were the two major advances in land transport. Domesticated animals are used for packing, for draft, and for riding. The two main types of traction device are sliding vehicles and wheeled vehicles.

Overland transport in difficult country frequently depends on using peculiarly well adapted domesticated animals. The husky dog, with its remarkable powers of endurance and resistance to sub-zero temperatures is an excellent example of such an animal. There are more than a dozen different breeds, all more or less adapted to specific local conditions and requirements. The yak, which, like the South American llama, can withstand severe cold and high altitudes, is the indispensable beast of burden in Tibet. In arid desert tracts the endurance powers of the one-humped Arabian camel, which is used both for riding and as a pack animal, are justly famed. The camel's toes are broad and spreading so that it does not easily sink into soft sand. Donkeys and mules are even more widely found in the peasant world as pack and riding animals. The mule is also particularly useful in the tropics.

Riding an animal may or may not involve the use of a saddle. Many people who use a saddle do not use other devices normally associated with saddles, such as stirrups. Some animals, such as the donkey or horse, normally carry one rider. The camel or Indian elephant can carry several.

The *travois* is a simple sliding vehicle used by the Plains Indians of North America. It consists principally of two poles joined together and harnessed to the shoulders of a dog or horse. The load is borne on a platform or hoop attached to the poles, with its weight supported by the ground. Sledges and sleds are used not only on snow and ice, but also on slippery or even on dry ground. The sledge differs from the sled in that it has no runners, but moves on a flat bottom. The Lapps are renowned for their fast-moving reindeer sledges. Sleds, which are used throughout the boreal zone, come in many different types, according to the purpose for which they are designed. The Eskimo sled drawn by a team of huskies, harnessed so that either one pair runs behind the other on a single trace (in forest country) or each pair runs on a separate trace (in open country) is a highly efficient traction device. The Eskimo have ingenious methods for minimizing friction. They blow water from the mouth over the runners, for example, to create a film of ice over the edge of each runner.

In regions where there are no paved roads and wide bridges, or over rough or muddy ground, wheeled vehicles are often less efficient than some of the transport devices described above. The wheelbarrow of Chinese civilization, however, is designed for hilly areas on narrow tracks, and in the Pripet Marshes of Poland partly submerged horse-drawn carts negotiate the relatively firm beds of streams which run through the marshes. Large parts of North America and Australia were 'opened up' by the horse- and ox-drawn waggon.

Using wheeled vehicles is often associated with the growth of big sedentary populations, and large-scale trade between urban settlements. Oxen, which were probably among the earliest draft animals, are widespread. Before the advent of motor vehicles ox- and horse-drawn carts and carriages were principal freight and passenger vehicles in Europe and elsewhere. The demise of the horse-drawn cart in the face of competition from the motor car in rural England is beautifully portrayed in Grahame's *The Wind in the Willows* where Toad's canary colored cart is smashed by an early road hog.

The wheel is supposed to have originated in the region of the Tigris-Euphrates, and to have diffused thence throughout the civilized world. Although there has been much academic speculation about contribution of 'the wheel' to the evolution of past and present civilizations which have drawn into the discussion quite different rotary devices such as the potter's wheel – it must be remembered that the vehicular wheel is a complex artifact of at least four main types. There is the solid wheel fashioned from a single log of wood; the plank-built composite disc; the rim supported on a square frame; and the wheel with a central nave from which spokes radiate to the outer rim. Often a considerable amount of craftsmanship is involved in wheel-making and the production of the fourth kind of complex wheel requires the skills of a specialist wheelwright.

Water provides the sole effective medium for transport in many environments, such as impenetrable forest or archipelagos. Some of the simplest water transport devices are swimming floats of bamboo or a pot, and rafts made of reeds or logs. Two types of ocean-going raft have received world-wide publicity as a result of the maritime adventures of Thor Heyerdahl: the balsa raft on which he sailed from the Peruvian coast to the Tuamotu Islands in Polynesia, and the papyrus raft which carried him from Morocco to Barbados. These are highly developed forms of log and reed rafts, and in their simpler versions are widely distributed in the world. The *catamaran* is, strictly speaking, a boat-shaped log raft of the Madras coast. Its name is derived from a Tamil expression for 'tied together'.

There are many varieties of simple hollow vessels – from bark boats and skin-covered boats to dugout canoes. There are bark vessels in parts of Australia, the Americas, eastern Asia and Africa. The craft of bark canoe construction reached its height among such Amerindian tribes as the Yakut, Tungus, and Yahgan. In a bark canoe the wooden frame is pegged and tied, and covered with sections of bark finely sewn together. Bark

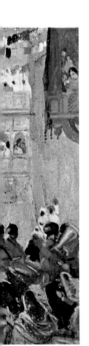

canoes are light and can be carried for long distances.

The kayak, used by the Eskimo seal hunter and noted for its great maneuverability, is one of the best known forms of skin-covered boat. The kayak is constructed from a wooden or whalebone frame covered with seal skins. It is equipped with a skin cover over the cockpit gunwales which draws tightly around the waist of the paddler, who uses a double or single paddle. The Eskimo also have the umiak, a larger open boat covered with seal skin which they use for whale-hunting and for traveling – and propel with oars. Loops of rawhide form rowlocks.

There are coracles in many parts of the world, including India, central Asia, and Britain. In north America coracles, termed 'bull boats', were used on the Missouri river, fashioned from willow sticks covered with buffalo skin. The three Welsh rivers of the Teifi, Towy and Taf today comprise the principal areas where the coracle survives in Britain. Until recently it was much more extensively distributed, especially in Wales and England. Coracles are still used for salmon fishing in Wales. The frame is woven from willow or ash sticks, and the skin is nowadays of tarred and pitched canvas. Raymond Rees of Carmarthen is a prominent coracle craftsman and fisherman.

At Ironbridge, in Shropshire in England, Eustace Rogers produces coracles of the bowl shaped Severn type. He is the last in a long line of English coracle makers. Ironbridge coracles are made of sawn ash lathes covered with calico soaked in a special tar and pitch mixture. They were used for poaching along the river banks, and for fishing. Mr Rogers has also produced willow-framed coracles covered with bullock hide secured to the frame with horse hair twine – full-scale replicas of the extinct Scottish Spey type.

Coracles are propelled by a single paddle used over the front of the vessel in a characteristic 'figure-of-eight' motion which pulls rather than pushes them through the water. They are normally carried upstream on the back. In Ireland there are *curraghs,* or sea-going boats covered with tarred canvas. The larger ones are rowed or sailed instead of paddled.

Although since World War II there has been a drastic decline in the number of traditional British coracle men because of the scarcity of their customary catch, the salmon, there is some indication that the coracle will not become entirely defunct in the near future. Scattered throughout the country are many coracle enthusiasts, some of whom have innovated in coracle design and materials. On the Teifi at Cilgerran near Cardigan the 'Coracle Races and Aquatic Sports' have been held annually for over two decades, providing an event of increasing tourist interest. Both coracles and *curraghs* have appeared in various boat shows in recent years, and there is at least one commercial coracle producer. Perhaps we are witnessing the beginning of a transformation of the coracle from a utilitarian artifact to an article of popular entertainment.

Dugout canoes are found virtually wherever there is a supply of large enough timber. A log is usually hollowed out by using wedges and adzes and controlled burning, and may be shaped after it is hollowed by heating it and inserting supporting beams. The height of the hull may be increased by fixing a plank or planks along the top of the dugout portion of the hull to make a 'wash-strake'. Unfinished canoe hulls are frequently traded from areas which have supplies of suitable timber to those which do not. The north-west coast Amerindians produced huge cedarwood canoes capable of undertaking voyages of hundreds of miles in the open sea. There is a great variety of dugout canoes in Oceania, including the simple dugout, double and multi-hulled vessels, and single and double outrigger canoes. The outrigger is essentially a stabilizing device secured at some distance from, and in line with, the hull, on boom-poles. The single outrigger canoe can be paddled or sailed. When sailed the outrigger is always kept to windward, so that when tacking against the wind the rigging is periodically reversed and the prow of the boat becomes the stern, and vice versa as required.

In parts of Oceania in particular, canoe building is the work of groups of craftsmen who are exponents of the technical and ritual expertise which are necessary to produce traditional craft. The canoe is then rarely regarded as a mere transport device, but as an object of chiefly or communal ownership and inheritance. In many areas, including the Solomon Islands, canoe houses are focal points for social and ceremonial purposes.

Although many Oceanic peoples, especially the Polynesians, are great navigators, certain hypotheses concerning the colonization of the far-flung coral atolls by flotillas of intrepid sailors voyaging into the unknown with the aid of now forgotten navigating devices such as the sacred calabash have acquired a romantic aura. Accidental colonization by primitive mariners blown off course has, in all probability, played a significant part in populating the Pacific islands.

Plank-built boats fall into two basic groups according to whether they are carvel-built or clinker-built. In the clinker-built hull the planks overlap, as in the classic example of the Viking ship. Another dual classification is into shell and skeletal methods of construction. The frames are added afterwards in shell construction while the planks are built upon a supporting frame according to the skeletal method. In non-metal-using cultures which do not use nails, planks may be secured by pegging or by stitching with fiber through holes bored in the planks, and then caulked with a waterproof substance.

Propelling watercraft by exploiting the wind is generally more efficient than paddling or rowing. Most smaller vessels, however, carry paddles or oars as well as sails, for example, to use when a dugout canoe has to be paddled out over a heavy surf before proceeding under sail in the open sea. Square or crab-claw varieties of sail are a common means of propulsion among vessels in many parts of the world. The techniques of sailing reached a high level of sophistication in the large plank-built craft of the voyages of discovery and trade on which the modern world of commerce is founded.

Today the few relatively 'untouched' regions do not have to be explored entirely by water, on foot, or with the aid of local devices, as in the explorations of the last few centuries. A new breed of compact versatile motorized vehicles has been developed. These include 'snow-cats', 'skidoos', amphibious automobiles and hovercraft. Increasing contact with the modern world is of course affecting traditional devices and systems of transport in some of the remotest areas. In Eskimoland individual motorized sleds are replacing the husky-drawn variety. In many parts of the world outboard motors are attached to dugout canoes. A pontoon can be constructed by joining together several dugout hulls and covering them with a platform capable of carrying heavy goods across rivers.

These changes often acquire a distinctive local character. In the Philippines, for example, the abandoned American jeep is pressed into service for local transport as the 'veepney' and it is here also that the tricycle and rickshaw have combined to produce the 'trishaw'. In the flat, low-lying land of the Ibibio of south-east Nigeria, the most popular modern transport device is the bicycle. Petty traders with pots of palm-wine, live goats, sewing machines and coffins tied behind their saddles ply the roads and bush tracks, and bicycle taxis bear people shaded by umbrellas on their carriers. Some men are specialists who respond to the call 'cyclist!' in the manner of the London cabman to that of 'taxi!' There are fixed rates of payment between each taxi 'drop', and in a town such as Uyo on busy market days there are virtual traffic jams of cyclists. Parked on its scrap-metal stand the bicycle provides an elevated view at the football match. Old bicycle spokes are hammered flat to make chords for 'thumb pianos' or African *sansas,* and wheel-chain-pedal

A painted cart from Sicily. All forms of transport have a secondary function as status objects. This cart would enhance its owner's social standing.

units are converted into bellows used by local blacksmiths.

The 'mammy-waggon' or beat-up lorry is the chief means of public transport outside the cities in Nigeria. These gaily-painted vehicles bear signs such as 'VC 10' and 'Lord help us'. In the west animal sacrifices are made on vehicle bonnets and bumpers. It is propitious to run over a dog and an ill omen to kill a duck in the road. The Yoruba wood carvers in Nigeria are adept at incorporating representations of bicycles, cars and lorries into both traditional and contemporary art forms. Old ancestral screens of the Niger delta area include models of European sailing vessels of the type used in the slave and palm-oil trade of the 18th and 19th centuries.

As in other aspects of culture, devices and methods of transport do not only serve utilitarian requirements. In many cases certain beliefs and values are expressed in them. There was an obvious status difference, for example, between the passengers and porters of a sedan chair. Riding behind silk curtains in a *howdah* on the back of a bejeweled elephant was largely the prerogative of the Indian royalty. Among the nomadic Beduin the horse is generally ill adapted to desert conditions and is used only for raiding and as a prestige item for chiefs. Among the Kazakh of central Asia expert horsemanship occupies a vital position in their value-system. They wear riding boots that are difficult to walk in, and much wealth is invested in horse trappings. In Texas the hat and boots derived from the cowboys' traditional apparel are worn by men who nowadays drive around in Ford trucks rather than ride horses. In many instances 'the journey' itself acquires a special meaning, as when it symbolizes the transition from one status or role to another in some form of rite of passage. Examples include the Muslim *haj* to Mecca, Christian pilgrimages, and the canoe voyages in the Bay of Bengal of youths from the island of Car Nicobar to Chowra, which constitutes a test of manhood related to the puberty rites of the Nicobarese male.

Only in a very few areas of the world have primitive communities remained completely isolated for long periods of time. Elsewhere there has been a more or less constant interflow of people, goods, and hence ideas, which has had far-reaching effects on cultural development. Perhaps the extreme cultural poverty of the Tasmanian aborigines was related to their unusual detree of geographic isolation.

(Over page) Los Angeles. Early transport was adapted to suit the land. Now the land is altered to accommodate vehicles.

# Man the traveler

## Islamic/Semitic world

Qashqa'i tribesmen, like all desert nomads of the middle east, rely heavily on the camel for food, transport and by-products like skins. Although it is not true that camels can survive on little water (they need, in fact, large quantities in proportion to their body weight) their range — between drinks — exceeds that of any other domestic animal.

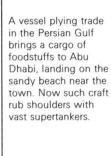

A vessel plying trade in the Persian Gulf brings a cargo of foodstuffs to Abu Dhabi, landing on the sandy beach near the town. Now such craft rub shoulders with vast supertankers.

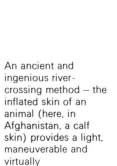

An ancient and ingenious river-crossing method — the inflated skin of an animal (here, in Afghanistan, a calf skin) provides a light, maneuverable and virtually unsinkable craft.

## Central and northern Asia

Recalling the cavalry prowess of their Mongol forbears, who nearly overran Christian Europe, this decorated saddle is still in use among the Kirghiz tribesmen of central Asia. It is carved from a single piece of wood and ornamented with beaten leather and camel bone.

Still magnificent horsemen, the one million Mongols share a country the size of western Europe with 23 million domestic animals — a large proportion of them horses.

The reindeer, pictured here in Siberia, is used throughout the Arctic zones of Europe and Asia as a pack animal and food source.

## Southern Asia

A small boy of the Bajau Laut in the Philippines uses stilts to negotiate the shallow waters in which the family houseboat (the Bajau home) is moored.

A leg rower on Lake Inle, Burma, propels his boat through the shallow waters of the lake. The rower stands on one leg in the stern and hooks his other leg round the oar, using his own body as a pivot.

The yoke, in one form or another, is a widespread and efficient method of carrying heavy loads. Here a Thai farmer carries a load of rambutan fruit to market.

## Western-dominated world

The world-famous Venetian gondola evolved through the centuries to ply the canals of Venice. Now used entirely as a taxi for visitors, the gondola was originally designed to carry goods as well.

Still to be seen in the west of Ireland, and once the staple form of transport in rural Britain — the pony trap.

Perhaps the commonest and cheapest form of personal transport — the bicycle, ridden here by a Dutch woman wearing her traditional clogs.

Black Africa

Australasia

For centuries man's foremost method of transport in commerce and war, the horse has now been superseded. Even in areas like the Muslim emirates of Cameroun, where the use of the horse is still widespread, this mount finds itself relegated to ceremonial duties.

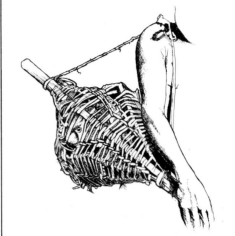

Going to market, with a difference. (Top) A man carries a *cuscus*, a valuable tree-dwelling marsupial, to Gumine in the central highlands of New Guinea. Unlike a European market, however, goods are exchanged in kind, not sold for cash. The cage is made from a single split bamboo. (Below) Women carry pandanus fruit to Gumine in net bags made of fibers.

A cushy job? An Ethiopian camel driver sits on top of a consignment of mattresses being transported by his camels.

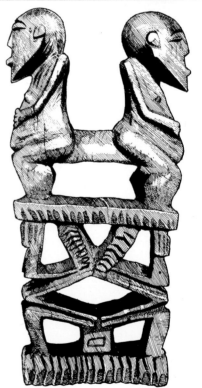

This decorative piece of statuary from Tahiti is used as a canoe paddle rest.

Sitting astride his alert-looking pony a young tribesman of north Dahomey sets out on a hunting trip. He rides bareback with no stirrups recalling the early days of man's domestication of the horse before these refinements were invented. Only with the development of the saddle and stirrups did it become possible for rider and horse to act in full unison, and, more important still, for the rider to exchange blows with foe or quarry from the back of a moving horse.

## Amerindia

A typically stylized dog-faced wooden stirrup used until recently by the Gauchos of Argentina and Paraguay. Decorated with characteristic Guarani carvings, the stirrup is encircled by an inlaid metal band. Height: 15 cm.

American Polar bear hunters use an Eskimo sled, pulled by twelve husky dogs. In heavy going the runners have to be iced every 3 to 5 hours to make them run smoothly.

A Naskapi Indian from Labrador wears snowshoes. By spreading his weight, snowshoes enable him to cross surfaces that would not otherwise bear his weight.

## Orient

Once popular in the far east, but rarely seen now, the tricycle rickshaw enabled the cyclist to carry two passengers.

The litter, sedan chair and rickshaw all used muscle power to carry the privileged rider about.

A father pushes his children in a makeshift pram in Peking.

# Man the traveler

## Islamic/Semitic world

The long-suffering donkey. Tough, tenacious and on occasions wholly bloody-minded, donkeys have served mankind as the poor man's horse throughout Europe, Asia and north Africa, for thousands of years.

A Tuareg woman roosts in her palanquin on top of her camel. The lightweight platform balances on a camel saddle and can be curtained off from view.

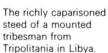

The richly caparisoned steed of a mounted tribesman from Tripolitania in Libya.

## Central and northern Asia

A bridge over the River Muksu in Soviet central Asia demonstrates one ancient and simple method of solving the problems of spanning a spate river. If the bridge is to be permanent, all parts of it must be clear of the flood level of the river bed. In this case overlapping log sections have been built high on the banks, extending far enough over the river to carry the main spar, two logs covered with planks.

Taken on the Norwegian, Finnish and USSR borders, this picture shows Lapps traveling in the time-honored Father Christmas style — by reindeer sledge. The whole Lapp economy revolves round the reindeer (the old world equivalent of the North American caribou) on which they depend not only for transport, but for hides, bone and meat.

A camel-drawn carriage from Ulan Bator, Mongolia, which also boasts, in sharp contrast to these wooden-wheeled carts, a modern airport.

## Southern Asia

An Indian in the river estuary at Madras fishes from his primitive cane and log craft. As his needs do not extend beyond a floating platform to fish from, these craft have remained unaltered for centuries.

A Sherpa in Katmandu employs a time-honored method of carrying a load. A back-pack (wider at the top than the bottom to ensure a high ride for the load) is additionally supported by a headband that allows the wearer to take some of the strain with his neck muscles.

Half the population of Saigon lives on the water, and many conduct their business on it as well, like these Vietnamese peddling their wares from their boats.

## Western-dominated world

'What is this that roareth thus? Can it be a motor bus?' Godley's famous verse captured much of the mingled affection and irritation in which Englishmen hold the backbone of their urban public transport system, the double-decker bus.

This Boeing 747 Jumbo jet, capable of carrying over 300 passengers, represents a major development in air travel. Throughout the history of civil aviation speed has vied with capacity. The number of Jumbo jets in service represents a temporary victory of capacity, while supersonic projects languish at the prototype stage.

In many ways the ideal means of passenger transport, helicopters provide the advantages both of aircraft and vehicles. The snag? High running costs.

# Man the traveler

Built for Thor Heyerdahl of *Kon Tiki* fame, the reed craft *Ra* is shown here under construction in Chad, the only remaining location of the reeds that Heyerdahl believes may have been used in the first translantic voyages by the Phoenicians.

A Konjo woman from the Mountains of the Moon in Ruwenzori carries her load supported by a head band. As forest dwellers the Konjo find the normal African method of carriage, balancing on the head, inconvenient. The basket, made of vines collected from the Ituri forest by pygmies, holds goat and monkey skins from which the Konjo make clothes.

Tananarive, the capital of Madagascar, is a city of canals surrounded by the wetlands of the central Madagascar plateau. Its inhabitants are believed to be of Polynesian descent, and this dugout canoe, still in common use amongst them, has similarities with those of the Pacific.

The outrigger principle, widely used to provide stability to slender craft without reducing their speed through the water, originated in the Pacific islands. Here islanders of New Caledonia paddle an outrigger canoe.

A group of men in north east Arnhemland Australia, construct a bark canoe from a single piece of bark. The outside of the bark becomes the inside of the canoe, and the ends are sewn together with vines. A pole is laced down each side at the gunwale for rigidity.

Fishing rafts used in the Philippines have nets suspended from twin booms supported by an A-frame anchored on a pivot to the deck.

## Amerindia

The dugout, possibly the most ancient form of water transport, is, by itself, inherently unstable and requires great skill on the part of its occupants. Many forest-dwelling people with access to large reserves of suitable timber still use dugouts, and those who use them in the sea where their instability would be too dangerous, often improve their performance by lashing two hulls together. The principle is the same as the outrigger.

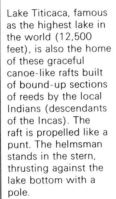

Lake Titicaca, famous as the highest lake in the world (12,500 feet), is also the home of these graceful canoe-like rafts built of bound-up sections of reeds by the local Indians (descendants of the Incas). The raft is propelled like a punt. The helmsman stands in the stern, thrusting against the lake bottom with a pole.

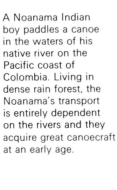

A Noanama Indian boy paddles a canoe in the waters of his native river on the Pacific coast of Colombia. Living in dense rain forest, the Noanama's transport is entirely dependent on the rivers and they acquire great canoecraft at an early age.

## Orient

Neither a wheelbarrow nor a rickshaw, this strange pushcart was pictured in China at the turn of the century. Carrying a pig on one side and a passenger on the other, its 'payload' must have been uncomfortably high for the pusher at the back.

Both overcrowding and a long tradition of life afloat induce a large number of Chinese in Hong Kong to live in boats. They may, as in this case, be small craft housing a single family, or they may have room for as many as 32 people. The craft serve both as a home and a place of business.

The junk, still a common sight in far eastern waters. Its three-masted rig, with rib-stiffened sails, gives efficient close-to-the-wind performance for inshore sailing.

# Man the fighter, man the hunter

From the age of discovery until the establishment of the colonial empires the Europeans who were in closest contact with the tribes and nations of Africa, Asia, Oceania, and the new world were the military and the merchants. Both groups had professional interests in the arms of the peoples amongst whom they worked and fought, and weapons were inevitably a popular memento of their travels. Over the years their cabinets of curiosities have found their way into the museums of the west, there to gather dust in storerooms and tempt curators to try their hand at classification. A study of firearms led a famous anthropologist, General Pitt-Rivers, to propose his theory of typological evolution.

Although infinitely diverse in details of form and decoration, weaponry shows less gross variation from continent to continent than many other classes of material culture, and it is less tied to environmental circumstances than, for example, types of houses or agricultural implements. The causes are not far to seek: the majority of weapons are portable and, whether as booty or items of commerce, can pass from hand to hand and from people to people. The steel tomahawk, so firmly identified with the American Indian, is of course a European import. Flesh and blood are much the same the whole world over; weapons proven in war or chase are copied and become widely distributed. The bow and arrow, thought to have been invented in north-east Africa or the near east some 15,000 years ago, had reached all but Australia by the time of first European contact. Nevertheless, if comparability of functional requirements and the diffusion of objects and ideas have led to broad-scale similarities in weaponry, yet there is significant variation. This variation is tied not so much to the culture area or to the environment as to the kind of economy, and to the level of technology and of social development of the society. Hunter-gatherers and food-producers have different armories, and knowledge of metallurgy leads to the production of new types of arms. The arsenals of states differ in quality and quantity from those of the simpler peoples.

The weapons of hunter-gatherers are light and easy to carry, of offense rather than defense, and of low mechanical efficiency. Unless, like the horsemen of the North American plains, they have means of transport, or, like the Indians of the north-west coast, access to rich and localized resources that make it possible to live in permanent settlements, hunters are nomads who cannot encumber themselves with equipment. With few exceptions they are thinly scattered over their territories and have little need or opportunity for internecine fighting. They may have no weapons of defense at all or they may be limited to a light shield or parrying-stick. The hunting band cannot support craft specialists and so, among all his other tasks, each man must make his own tools and weapons. By hacking with an unworked stone, hammering and wedging, a Pitjendajara Australian

splits a section off a living tree. He must then cut it roughly into shape and spend many tedious hours scraping it into the elegant curved form of the *wummera,* an appliance that combines the functions of spear-thrower, carrying dish and haft for a scraper-adze, and, sawed back and forth across a shield, will also be used to make fire. Although an accomplished workman, the hunter is naturally less skilled than a professional full-time craftsman and must compensate for the feebleness of his weapons by his vast knowledge of the territory and of its animal and plant resources.

Beyond the tropics, where man originated, a greater mechanical skill is needed to adapt to harsh environments. We may contrast the ingenious harpoons and hunting devices of the Eskimo with the much simpler bows and spears of the Congo pygmies. But, from vegetable juices and the venom of snakes and insects, the hunters of the warmer regions have learned to concoct powerful poisons that add immeasurably to the effect of their puny weapons.

All hunters use clubs, of bone and walrus ivory among the Eskimo, but more usually of wood with knobs or swellings at the head to give power to the blow. The Plains Indians add a stone wrapped in a rawhide pouch. Clubs used as missiles tend to be curved and flattened, and reach their most advanced form in the Australian aboriginals' *boomerang,* which they use in games and to bring down birds especially over water. To finish off a wounded animal or as protection against a predator hunters often carry a heavy spear or lance. They throw

lighter darts or javelins to wound and kill. Their spears may be of one piece with the tip worked to a point by charring and scraping, but since straight growing woods are rarely hard enough, spearheads are usually made of bone or of chipped flakes of obsidian, quartzite or flinty rocks. Projectile points are attached to the shaft by vegetable gum or beeswax and lashed with thongs or fibers. For fishing and fowling spears with multiple points are often used; tridents, salmon leisters, and eel spears are still in use in Europe. Various technical devices ensure that the point or points remain in the wound to cause maximum damage. The spear- or arrow-head may be barbed or fixed to a detachable foreshaft. Harpoons, used 16,000 years ago in western Europe for hunting reindeer, are mainly used today to catch fish and aquatic mammals. The head of the harpoon which is sunk in a slit or socket, comes away from the shaft on impact but remains attached by a line either to a float or to the shaft itself. In the most developed Eskimo toggle-head type of harpoon the line passes through the middle of the head. Once this is embedded in the prey it is pulled around by the drag of the line and offers maximum resistance to extraction. The walrus or seal tires quickly and comes to the surface where it is clubbed or stabbed to death.

By adding length to the arm, the spear-thrower, which may be flexible but is more often made with a rigid stick or slat, gives increased leverage and power. The *ounep* of New Caledonia is a short length of cord with a loop for the index finger and, at the other end, a hook or knot which is hitched around the middle of the spear, and disengages at the moment of release. A peg on the *wummera* fits into the butt of the spear. In northern New Guinea bamboo spear-throwers are provided with a socket. These and other devices are found in the new world together with shaped grips for the hand. The hand-grips of the Eskimo are especially finely carved for precise control under icy conditions.

The bows and arrows of hunter-gatherers are no more superior in range and little more accurate than spears projected by a spear-thrower. Neither device is in fact commonly used at ranges greater than 30-40 yards. But bows and arrows do have several other advantages. Bows are easier to fire from confined spaces and arrows can be aimed upwards. The loss of an arrow is less serious as it is relatively easy to replace and more and more varied projectiles can be carried, suited to the game that the hunter is likely to encounter.

The bow, in the brief moment before the release of the arrow, represents man's first achievement in the mechanical storage of energy. In its simplest form it is fashioned from a single piece of elastic wood, with a bowstring made of rawhide, sinew, strips of rattan or twisted fiber. The length and shape of the stave depends on the available materials and on the technique of construction. African bows are made of resilient woods and are generally short, while the palm-wood bows of the tiny Semang of the Malayan forests or of the Siriono of Bolivia must be made six to nine feet long to give sufficient recoil. Hunters in northern coniferous forests and plains of both the old and the new worlds reinforce their bowstaves by glueing or lashing lengths of sinew on to the back of them. When the bow is unstrung it takes a reflex curve with the ends pointing away from the archer. Where wood is scarce or of very poor quality, as among the Cheyenne or Eskimo, reflex bowstaves are built up of bits of wood, bone, antler or horn, lashed together and backed with sinews to strengthen them.

Where there are no tough reeds, no bamboo, and no woods like hazel that grow naturally straight, arrow shafts must be cut from thin branches. The Selknam of Tierra del Fuego scrape down their arrows with a mussel shell, then polish them on a sandstone block, and finally straighten them by heating the wood, using their teeth as clamps. A heavy hard-wood foreshaft improves accuracy, as do flights of feathers, leaves or occasionally skin. Arrowheads may be leaf-shaped, tanged, or tri-angular, and made of wood, bone or stone. Many peoples make blunt arrowheads to stun birds and small animals without damaging the feathers or fur. Arrows with multiple points, like modern shot-guns, give a better chance of hitting small game. The Buriat of Siberia and other northern peoples sometimes fix a whistle behind the arrowhead. The game is surprised by the sound and stands still till the arrow has found its mark.

Other weapons are best suited to particular environ-ments. The *bolas,* for example, is a weapon of open country. The Puelche of the Argentinian pampas make *bolasses* of two or three stone balls. These are either grooved or wrapped in hide so that they can be attached to each other by leather thongs. The *bolas* is whirled around the head and thrown. The balls spin apart and the thongs entangle the legs of the game, rhea bird or guanaco. A smaller version of *bolas* with several weights is used by the Eskimo to bring down birds in flight. The blowgun on the other hand, is a weapon of the tropical forests of South-east Asia and South America. It is used from these parts of the world to Madagascar and to the area of the Cherokee and Iroquois in the eastern wood-lands of North America. The tube of the gun varies in length from five to twenty feet – always excluding the schoolboy's peashooter – and it can be made in several ways. The Malayan Sakai blowgun has an inner tube made of two lengths of bamboo, supported by a stronger bamboo outer tube. To this is attached a funnel-shaped mouthpiece which was formerly of wood but is now of metal. The missiles may be clay pellets, but are more usually tiny splinters of bamboo, their butts stuck into light plugs of pith shaped to fit the bore, and their tips dipped in a poison so toxic that just one will kill an elephant – if the hunter can shoot sufficiently accurately enough to hit it in the eye. As the blowgun is powered 101 only by air compressed in the human lungs it can only be a short-range weapon, but the darts do have the advantage of being freely expendable.

The consequences of producing – whether by agriculture or animal husbandry – rather than hunting and gathering food, include denser populations and larger, more permanent and socially differentiated communities. These differences in way of life are reflected in the weaponry of these societies as in other aspects of their material culture. But unless a society can also use metals, new inventions are rare. And changes in their weaponry are mainly due to improvements in production techniques and organization and to the marked increase in warfare which follows competition for land and other resources. In New Guinea a large cane loop on a pointed wooden shaft is used to capture a fleeing enemy. Pastoral and other peoples living in open plains have lassos and slings. Battle axes and club-heads of stone which require painstaking, lengthy grinding into shape, make their appearance.

In Fiji, and in other parts of Oceania, wooden clubs are made by professional craftsmen. They are artists, some of whom were attached to chiefly households, who take pride in fine workmanship. Carving and decoration sometimes with ivory inlay, and polishing the most valued clubs takes days or weeks. Months, even years, were spent in tending the roots of saplings so that they took the shape appropriate for the *waka,* a club with root-stumps left as projections from the head. The many different types of clubs they made include spiked stabbers, pole clubs shaped like baseball bats for the smashing downward blow, and clubs with well-developed spurs for pecking through the skull. Perfectly symmetrical clubs are made for throwing, others specially to use when dancing and yet others for funerals and ceremonies. Clubs that had killed many men were sacred.

Using metals has further important implications. Smiths, as they are customarily full-time specialists, are correspondingly experts. Because they make deadly weapons, the smiths of the Masai, who form a hereditary inter-marrying caste, are despised. The smiths of their neighbors the Chagga, on the other hand, are feared and honored. Among the Lamba and other Bantu peoples of central and southern Africa smithing is a respected and lucrative profession learned by many chiefs. Metal tools make it possible to manufacture complex weapons more easily and more productively. Making the sophisticated reflex bow, for example, which is used over most of western and northern Asia was never attempted without the aid of metal tools. These, the most powerful known bows, are built up of plates of horn, bone, wood and sinew, all glued together and completed by an ornamental covering of birchbark or lacquer. They are sometimes signed by the maker. The bows used by the horsemen of the Asiatic steppes are short and their reflex curve is so marked that when the bow is unstrung

the ends may meet.

Everywhere that copper, bronze or iron are generally available they have replaced the more primitive forms of axe-, spear- and arrow-head. They have also encouraged the development of new types of weapons such as the war-flail of China and medieval Europe, the light battle-axe of parts of India and Africa, and the elaborate copper spears of the Congo. Metals have also led to a whole new family of fighting, rather than hunting, weapons, designed to complement the old functions of crushing and piercing with cutting and slashing. Stone knives and daggers are, it is true, found among many peoples who lack metallurgy, but then they are used primarily as tools. The sword-like clubs of the Gilbert Islanders, set with sharks' teeth, or those of the ancient Mexicans with inset obsidian blades, crack bones and lacerate rather than cut deep into the flesh.

While there are knives and sabers, with one cutting edge, and daggers and swords, which are sharp on both sides, all over the old world, in the major ethnographic areas of the world there tend to be marked preferences either for one-edged or two-edged weapons. In addition there is a superabundance of local types according to tribal fashion and styles of fighting. In the Islamic world and the orient sabers are far more common than swords. Some, like the Indian saber have heavy, convex cutting edges, while the lighter Turkish *yataghan* curves inwards and is used to thrust as well as cut. The Gurkha *kukri* is a combination machete-knife, and the long Japanese saber is a two-handed weapon that has not changed in form since the 7th century. Exotic types include the Indian thrusting dagger or *jamdhar* which has three blades which spring apart to parry an adversary's blow, and the flamboyant Indonesian *kris.* The *kris* hilt is typically crooked and the wavy blade is forged by welding iron and steel of different qualities together to give a patterned effect known as damascening – after Damascus, which was for long a center for the production of quality weapons.

Although the curved saber was borrowed in the middle ages for use by both cavalry and, as the cutlass, by the navy, daggers and swords are the preferred sidearms in Europe and Africa. In the 16th century as European swordsmen came to rely more on the point than on the edge, the light thrusting rapier was developed. Short broadswords are made in many curious forms in the Congo basin, some without points and others with forked or even crescent tips. The Chad-Congo watershed to the north is the center of distribution of the lethal African throwing knife. This weapon can take off a man's leg at twenty-five yards.

Improvements in offensive weaponry call for parallel advances in defense. These are leather jackets and helmets, and shields of basketry, wood and hide in many parts of the world. There may be an element of psychological warfare in the way that they are decorated. Some

On Pakistan's north-west frontier rifles are still produced in one-room factories — exact replicas of the originals.

of its budget to warfare than can a simpler society. Vast sums may be spent on research and development of new and more fearsome weapons. Since the appearance of the first primitive breech-loading cannon in the 14th century, gunpowder has conferred the capability of killing and maiming larger and larger numbers of people at ever increasing distances and at an ever diminishing risk to the men who fire the weapons.

The balance of forces is maintained by metal helmets and by body armor, of articulated plates in Europe, chainmail in the Islamic world and through Russia to Siberia, and of scales or platelets in the high cultures of the far east. Large, footed metal shields enabled the Japanese infantry to form a rampart against the enemy, while the cavalry tended to be equipped with maneuverable round shields for parrying. The mounts of the heavy cavalry – the military arm equivalent to our tanks – may themselves be clad in steel plate. Although scale armor has recently been revived in the form of the flak jacket, which has saved many lives in the Korean and Vietnamese wars, traditional armor gives little protection against effective firearms. The striking force of an arrow from a powerful bow is about twenty-five foot-pounds, as compared with the 2,445 foot-pounds of a bullet from a US Springfield rifle. But most hand-guns are very considerably less powerful and often quite unreliable, although they brought about many changes in strategy and tactics. Long-barreled, muzzle-loading muskets, which are the most widely distributed forms of hand-guns can be manufactured by a competent smith. The matchlock, which is triggered by the release of a slow-burning match onto the powder, is the gun of the east. Flintlocks which are ignited by sparks from a gunflint striking a steel plate, were carried to Africa in bulk in the days of the Slave Trade and are still in common use.

shields have magical designs to ward off harm from their bearers, others, like the war shield of the Borneo Kenyah-Kayan which are trimmed with human hair, are intended to destroy the enemy's morale. In other parts of south-east Asia the scales of the pangolin ant-eater are sewn together to make breastplates and helmets, and in the Gilbert Islands a complete – and surely excessively itchy – body armor is made of coconut husk fiber. Quilted cotton armor is characteristic of northern Africa and ancient Mexico and Peru.

Measures are taken to ensure collective security as well as to protect individuals. Calthrops or spikes, for example, may be strewn around the settlement. In Europe these are of metal. In Borneo and the Congo poisoned splinters of wood were set to hinder the enemy's advance. Villages are commonly fortified by walling and trenches, moats and thickets of thorn. The major achievements in this field in military engineering and of the siege train are, however, associated with societies which have a state level of political organization and a centralized military command that can call on an organized fighting force, if not on a standing army.

A state can afford to devote a far greater proportion

More important than the improvements in hand weaponry achieved by specialist armorers that follow the formation of states are developments in military organization. Shaka, ruler of the Zulu, for example, achieved overwhelming military superiority by forming his tribesmen into *impis* or regiments and arming them with short stabbing assegais in place of throwing spears. States can invest in chariots and catapults, in cannon, tanks and warships, and all the things that require major capital outlay both on the materials needed to make them and the professionals needed to man them. As weapons increase in power they become less and less selective in their effects. The cayenne pepper smoke-screens, used in Meso-America to drive defenders from their entrenchments, anticipate the use of poison gas. Bombs cannot distinguish between combatant and non-combatant and put only aircrews at risk. With guided missiles that can be fired from continent to continent to desolate vast areas, and may possibly render this planet uninhabitable to all mankind, we enter a new era in organized warfare. 103

(Over page) An Italian Macchi fighter plane at the 1971 Paris air show demonstrates the formidable armament of the modern warplane.

# Man the fighter, man the hunter

## Islamic/Semitic world

Tuareg horsemen of the Sahara carry rifles as well as more ancient weapons, the sword and the spear. Reared in a tradition of tribal skirmishing, they are formidable performers with all three.

Although the function of a gun butt imposes a similarity on their design all over the world, there are local variations in shape and decoration. This gun butt from North Africa, with a quadragonal cross section, is decorated with inlaid ivory strips. Length: 35 cm.

A Moroccan tribesman holds a flintlock musket. The trigger operates a hammer which strikes a piece of flint against a steel plate. This produces the spark which ignites the powder in the pan. Though still in use in a few Muslim countries the flintlock disappeared from European warfare in the 19th century.

## Central and northern Asia

To protect the head is a first need with all soldiers, but doubly so with mounted troops. The helmet has also a certain prestige and morale importance — can add to a man's height and lend an impression of ferocity. This cavalryman's helmet from central Asia has chain mail side flaps to guard the ears and neck.

The short, curved, powerful bow of Mongolia is still in use among the nomadic Mongol tribes. Thought to have been used first about 15,000 years ago the bow in one form or another remained man's most widespread missile-firing device until the introduction of gunpowder.

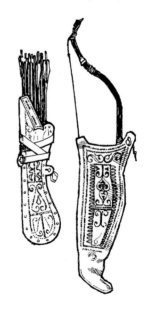

A quiver and bow holder from Mongolia used with the bow above.

## Southern Asia

A curved cutting knife, known as a *bolo*, still in use throughout southern Asia, is seen here with a carved handle shaped like a human fist.
Length: 45 cm.

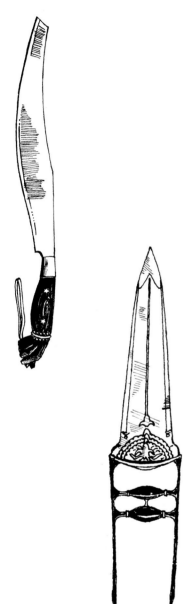

This decorative fishing spear-head from southern Asia is known locally as a *katar*. Length: 15 cm.

Temer aborigine tribesmen from Kelantan, Malaysia, use a log to cross a river. The men are carrying blow pipes, 180 cm long, made from a bamboo that grows only in the high mountains (at about 4,000 ft). Poison tipped darts up to 22 cm long are fired at birds, monkeys and other small game. There is a strong taboo against using blow pipes to kill men, a taboo only broken in the case of foreign invasion.

## Western-dominated world

On the earliest firearms, when only one shot at a time could be fired, some kind of stabbing weapon was needed as a follow up. A stabbing sword attached to the barrel, the bayonet, developed. The type illustrated here is a plug bayonet. It existed up to the 19th century, and had the grave disadvantage that it obstructed the barrel, preventing reloading and further firing while in use.

Not, as you might think, the spearhead of some World War I assault, but America's peace-keeping force. Military police parade at Fort Dix. They are armed with automatic rifles, bayonets, gas masks, and steel helmets.

Although inaccurate and useful only at short range, the hand-gun, or pistol, particularly the six chambered revolver, has been attributed a great deal of glamor fostered particularly by 'Wild West' myths of impossible marksmanship. The model shown here is a Smith and Wesson six chambered revolver. The 'revolver' principle appeared very early in the history of firearms, but came into its own only with the development of single charge and projectile cartridges in the late 19th century.

107

# Man the fighter, man the hunter

An Azante throwing knife from the Congo – many-bladed to increase the chances of a good hit. Length: 45 cm.

This arrowhead from the Besanti tribe of the Congo incorporates the 'barb' principle – a series of teeth below the striking point to ensure that the projectile remains stuck in the target. Length: 15 cm.

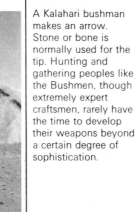

A Kalahari bushman makes an arrow. Stone or bone is normally used for the tip. Hunting and gathering peoples like the Bushmen, though extremely expert craftsmen, rarely have the time to develop their weapons beyond a certain degree of sophistication.

The world famous boomerang of the Australian Aborigines, possibly the most advanced form of throwing club. Its flattened surface below and curved surface above give it excellent aerodynamic properties, and the circular movement imparted by the thrower gives it its famous curved flight path. Length: 60 cm.

Tribesmen of the Chimbu highlands, New Guinea, offer a challenge to strangers approaching their village.

Another Aboriginal weapon is this spear projector. The spear is balanced in a trough-shaped piece of wood or bark which the hunter holds. As he jerks it down and forwards he gives considerable impetus to the spear.

## Amerindia

Two Tukano Indians with a hunting bow and a sheath of arrows. The curare-tipped arrows are protected from rain and damage by a carefully made sheath of cane and beeswax. The Tukano live along the River Piraparana in the north-west Amazon basin.

This wedge-shaped club from South America has a small stone head embedded in the 'business' end. Length: 30 cm.

The tomahawk, an axe weapon of the North American Indians. Length: 30 to 45 cm.

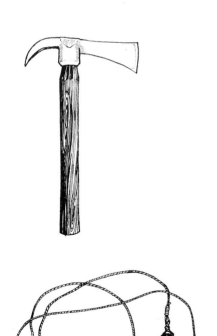

The *bolas*, Amerindia's most original weapon, was widely copied by the first Spanish settlers in South America. The weighted cords are swung and thrown to entangle a fleeing animal. Length: 90 to 120 cm.

## Orient

This bow case and quiver from the far east shows a similar origin to the Mongol case and quiver shown on page 106.

A tribesman of the unique Japanese tribe, the Ainu, raises his bow to fire an arrow. The Ainu are remarkable for their short powerful physique and the hairiness of their bodies. It is possible that the bow wielded by this tribesman is the prototype of the ceremonial bows used in Japanese archery.

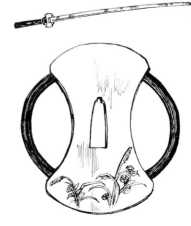

The manufacture of Japanese swords is wrapped in craft mystery. Their blades were built up by one of the most advanced tempering techniques in the world. Formerly the possession of a blade was the hallmark of a Samurai, a member of the Japanese warrior caste. Today Samurai swords bring prestige to collectors and specialists all over the world. The temper of these blades used to be tested by cutting through the bound bodies of seven convicted prisoners — all in one stroke. Today, a bundle of bolsters and timbers is used instead.

109

## Islamic/Semitic world

Possibly in no other part of the world has the art of war been practised more regularly and adeptly than in the Muslim dominated areas of the Mediterranean and central Asia. Here a tribesman of the north-west frontier of Pakistan (formerly the permanently embattled frontier of British India) rests his *jezail* on his knee. The *jezail*, a long barreled, muzzle-loading smooth bore, often has a bipod towards the front of the barrel to steady it for long-range shooting. When they can afford, or steal, an alternative, the tribesmen much prefer a modern, rifled weapon.

The blade structure of the cavalryman's saber is dictated by function, and is similar the world over. Here the hilt and hand-guard betray an Arabic, Muslim origin.
Length: 60 to 90 cm.

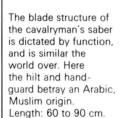

Two short side weapons from the Islamic countries. (Top) A short stabbing and cutting sword, similar to the deadly knives used with such effect against the invading British forces by the followers of the Mahdi in the Sudan during the 1890s. (Below) A curved dagger, a picturesque weapon most useful when used with an underhand upward thrust, point uppermost.
Length: 30 cm.

## Central and northern Asia

This 18th century Tibetan exorcising dagger is still used in Lamaist ritual for the slaying of the human effigy that represents the particular foe under attack. It is made of silver, and has a gem-studded handle that forms the greater part of its length. The short blade is triangular.
Length: 45 cm.

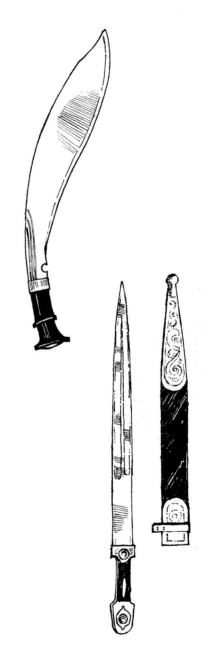

The world famous *kukri* of the Gurkhas of Nepal. Illustrated is the single-handed fighting knife. Its long curved cutting edge makes it a formidable weapon, and in the hands of a skillful user it can sever a human head from the body. A two-handed ceremonial *kukri* is used mainly at Dashera, the Gurkhas yearly religious festival when oxen and other domestic animals are sacrificially beheaded.
Length: 30 to 45 cm.

The *kinjal*, a straight-bladed, single-edged weapon from central Asia. Length: 60 cm.

## Southern Asia

The *bullova*, or light battleaxe, of southern Asia has a bow-shaped blade and long shaft. Length: 90 cm.

This elaborate Javanese shadow puppet depicts the background to the main action of a shadow play. The puppets, made of painted leather, are held up to the light producing a silhouette effect. Height: 40 cm.

The shield, used primarily to protect the bearer against blows, can have a secondary, psychological purpose. This example from Sarawak is decorated with human hair (in theory the hair of defeated enemies) in the form of a ferocious face to terrorize enemies. Height: 90 cm.

## Western-dominated world

All other weapons shown on this page could kill only one person at a time, but this nuclear-powered submarine carries the capability to destroy millions. Armed with a Polaris missile, the submarine can fire while still submerged. The target country has no method of knowing where the attack will come from, and no opportunity to pre-empt the attack by striking at the launching pad.

It did not take long for 20th century man to discover that his new-found toy, powered flight, was an ideal method of delivering destruction to his enemies. Thousands of types of bomb have been designed for this purpose, filled with high explosive, shrapnel or incendiary material. Some, like this, have been designed to burst on impact. Length: 60 cm.

The British Bloodhound surface to air guided missile is another example of industrial man's sophisticated weaponry. This is an entirely defensive weapon, designed to intercept and destroy nuclear missiles while still a safe distance from the target country. Length: 9 meters.

# Man the fighter, man the hunter

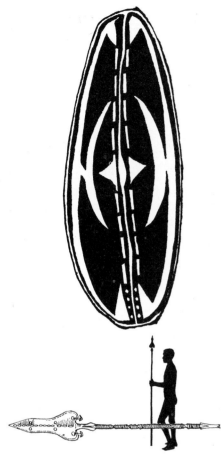

A shield used by the Masai of Kenya and Tanzania. A warlike, nomadic people, the Masai have resisted outside influence with more success than other tribes. Formerly their young warriors had to prove their manhood by killing a lion on foot with a spear. Length: 65 cm.

A Maori *patu*, or short club. (Below) Three *patu* rest on a feathered cloak. The nearest one is wooden, the two others are made of bone. The *patu* is a specialized weapon used primarily for hand to hand fighting. Length: 22 to 30 cm.

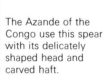

The Azande of the Congo use this spear with its delicately shaped head and carved haft.

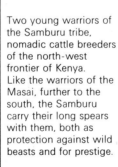

Two young warriors of the Samburu tribe, nomadic cattle breeders of the north-west frontier of Kenya. Like the warriors of the Masai, further to the south, the Samburu carry their long spears with them, both as protection against wild beasts and for prestige.

A shield from the New Guinea highlands again demonstrates the importance of decoration for psychological and religious purposes on military weapons. The intention is not only to protect the user, but to intimidate his enemies. Height: 90 cm.

Amerindia

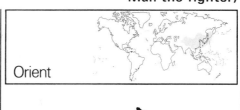

Orient

An arrowhead from Guyana, South America with a 'reversed' barb. The main point, thin and elongated, is backed up a few centimeters from the tip by five or six subsidiary points facing forwards and outwards. Such an arrowhead would be used against birds and other small quarry, and the barbs would secure a firmer grip on the prey and prevent the thick arrow shaft from penetrating its body and spoiling the meat. Length: 75 cm.

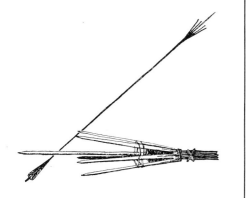

A two-handed executioner's sword from Japan.

Like the medieval knights of Europe, the Samurai of Japan armored not only their own persons, but their mounts as well. Here the armor to cover a horses' forehead and nose is shown.

South American Indians use a blowpipe to kill birds. The dart fired by a blowpipe could not, of itself, inflict a serious injury on any but the smallest target. Most blowpipe darts, therefore, are coated with one toxic substance or another to kill or knock out larger quarry.

This 19th century watercolor print from Japan, by the artist Kiniyoshi, shows two Samurai engaged in sword play. The swords of the Samurai were unique weapons, and today a good blade commands a high price for its antique value. Many of the secrets of the Japanese swordsmiths have been lost. Their methods of tempering steel and building up blades were entirely different from, and superior to, the European methods of the same era.

113

# Man the artist

Art is the aspect of a culture which possibly delights us more than anything else that people do. Through books and films, museums and galleries, – and by means of tourist flights – the art of the world becomes more and more readily available to us. And it is easy for us to appreciate. We do not need to be experts to feel uplifted by the delicate tracery of a gothic rose window, or twisted by the power and mystery of a Bangwa Night mask. But if we want to go beyond art's immediate appeal, we must look at it in its cultural context, rather than as merely a collection of museum exhibits. Our reward will be not only insight into the way of life of the people who produce the art, but also a correspondingly greater understanding of the art itself.

What art is really about is communication. It is first and foremost a means by which people express ideas and feelings about some element of their life. How can we know what is being communicated? We have to try to find out what the artist's symbols mean. For these symbols to have meaning there must be a sort of agreement between the artist and the people who 'read' his art. They must, in other words, share certain conventions of representation. When an Eskimo artist carves a highly distorted picture of a human face on a dance mask his Eskimo audience know at once that it is a spirit that is being represented because they know the convention. In all societies, modern as well as pre-industrial, it is only through conventions that anything can be experienced at all, but equally, in all societies, however strong the conventions, however unanimous the understanding of symbolism, there is always some scope for the artist to express his individualism. To understand the art of another society we must discover the extent of the artist's scope as well as the nature of the conventions. We must find out what the art means to the people who make and use it; what it is for; exactly what part it plays in their social organization and their economy, and, most importantly, in their religion.

Some previous approaches that have been made to this subject have stressed the sameness of both art and religion all over the world. It has been claimed that there is a 'universal aesthetic' – that all art can be compared in terms of its formal elements, harmony of proportion, balance of volumes and so forth, and that people from all cultures will find the same arrangements pleasing. There have likewise been theories of a universal attitude of awe which draws all religions together into one great category of worship.

The contrary viewpoint emphasizes the diversity of artistic and religious forms in the world. This is especially the approach of those who wish to make unfavorable comparisons between the supposedly enlightened and civilized cultures of western Europe and what have been called the 'primitive' peoples of the third world. How, they demand, can we possibly speak in the same breath of the glories of renaissance art and of African devil-

masks and fetishes? How can we compare the high-minded idealism of Christianity with the offering of sacrifices to pagan idols in an atmosphere of magic, sorcery and superstitious fear? Both of these approaches go too far. But there is an element of truth in both. Although the value-judgements of the second are ridiculous, it is true that the art of each culture is unique and works according to its own conventions, which cannot be understood in terms of the conventions of other cultures. The stress of the first approach, that the art of all cultures can be compared, is true in the sense that there is no unbridgeable gulf between western and 'primitive' art. But the basis of comparison is not a 'universal aesthetic'; it is the fact that art has certain functions in each society, and that these functions may vary as much between two 'primitive' societies as between a 'primitive' and a modern society.

Art does many things. In fact one of the surprising things about it is the number and diversity of its social roles, and this is true of the art of complex, industrialized societies as well as that of simple ones, as we shall see. One of the most widespread uses of art is to enhance religious ritual. To illustrate this, we will take a look at some of the most fascinating and beautiful art of North America: traditional Eskimo mask art. This art has largely disappeared as a living force in Eskimo culture. However, it is well represented in museums and art

114

Symbol of Mogul splendor, the Taj Mahal in Agra, northern India, immortalizes the love of 17th century Shah Jehan for his favorite wife.

publications, and it is of great interest to many people. The Eskimo of west Alaska are a hunting people who inhabit one of the harshest climatic regions in the world. Here immense skill and foresight are needed merely to survive. It is small wonder that these Eskimo did all they could to harness supernatural as well as natural forces to make their lives easier.

The Eskimo cosmos was inhabited by spirits and forces of various kinds – the spirits of food animals, of the sun and the moon, of various elemental forces that controlled the climate and the physical environment, personal guardian spirits, and shamans' helpers. All could be appeased and propitiated in order to improve those vital aspects of life over which the Eskimo had no direct control. The Eskimo's concern was notably to ensure a good supply of food animals, good weather in which to hunt them successfully, and freedom from unforseeable misfortune. Communication with the spirits was the job of the shamans, men and women who acted as intermediaries between the spirit world and the rest of society.

Festivals were held in special ceremonial houses, at which the shamans danced the dances of the various spirits. Beautifully carved and decorated masks were worn in order to represent more effectively to the people the animals, their spirits and other forces which they wished to thank or conciliate, and whose help and co-operation they wished to ask for. The people undoubtedly recognized the dancers, mask or no mask; but the masks added something extra which it was felt might move even the most difficult of spirits. They also represented the spirits to the people, making more effective communications between the two worlds possible through the medium of the shamans. Various conventions ensured that the people could readily identify the masks – for example, concentric rings made of roots fastened round a mask meant that another world was involved.

The environment, though harsh, provides the Eskimo with their food; masks play an important part in their attempt to influence that environment in their favor. The function of these Eskimo masks compares with the function of masks among a people who inhabit a more favorable latitude, the Yoruba of southern Nigeria. Their masking ceremonies are more concerned with social control and the maintainance of moral norms. Among the Eskimo, it is the environment that is the predominant constraining factor, rather than man-made social control mechanizations.

Traditional art may lose its original functions and meaning with the impact of the western world. It is a popular misconception that when this happens the art invariably loses its beauty and significance and becomes degenerate and worthless. But the case of modern Eskimo sculpture shows us that when the art loses its old meaning – the religious one – it may gain a new one. What is important is that there should still be an audience which shares some of the artist's conventions and, by meeting his work with certain expectations, understands it and sets standards for it. In the present-day sculpture, for example, of the Innuit Eskimo, who live in the Hudson's Bay area of northern Canada the art no longer has any religious significance, nor, as art, does it play any part in Innuit social life. Its usefulness as far as the Eskimo are concerned is purely economic; it is made for sale to shops and tourists; its ultimate destination lies entirely outside the Eskimo area. And yet these sculptures of men and birds and animals in soapstone and whalebone abound with vigor and originality. They are powerful and arresting and often brilliantly executed. The animals are portrayed with great sympathy, for Eskimo have a very clear understanding of the behavior of the animals they hunt. They associate a distinct personality with each species, and this is often detectable in the sculptor's treatment of seal, walrus, polar bear or whale. Now, it is this deep understanding of their environment which is the true thing these Eskimo have to say about themselves. Through the help and encouragement of a handful of sympathetic white people, who publicized their work and made constructive suggestions about style and subject matter and technical quality, the Eskimo can largely communicate this knowledge of their environment by means of their art to an enthusiastic and appreciative audience. Here we have an example of a people achieving a new audience for their art through the good offices of a sympathetic go-between.

Now let us return to our argument about similarities which may underlie the art of different cultures. Let us see if we can bring English and Camerounian into simultaneous focus, despite the fact that the works of art themselves appear ludicrously incompatible. We will take as our basis for comparing the two cultures the commissioning of art works for the enhancement of social and political status.

The Bangwa people, who live in the mountains of western Cameroun, are grouped into several independent chiefdoms, each with its complicated ranked hierarchy of chiefs, nobles, commoners and servants. As the supreme ruler of his chiefdom a Bangwa paramount chief may be very rich and powerful. As well as wealth in the form of death dues and marriage payments from his subjects, many symbols of his royal position, such as ivory tusks and leopard skins, enhance his status. Most important among these embellishments are the sets of carved wooden ancestor portraits which every chief should possess. On ritual occasions these figurines house the spirit of the ancestor they represent, and offerings are made to them. But they also function as a permanent testimonial to the chief's high status by providing him with a visible pedigree. A figurine is commissioned by the chief to be carved in his own likeness; and while it must suggest generalized chiefly attributes such as power and serenity, and must carry

115

standard emblems of royalty, it must also look as much like the sitter as possible. When the chief dies the figurine becomes his particular memorial and appears on public view at the death of every succeeding chief. High value is placed by the Bangwa on housing a complete set of ancestor portraits. In this context they can be compared with the ancestor portraits of our English aristocracy, which grace the dining halls of their descendants and similarly serve as visual evidence of their pedigree. In the not too distant past, when most of England was divided between these great families, such a display of status had as much political significance for the English as it does for the Bangwa. Although the ancestor portrait of a Bangwa paramount chief and that of an English nobleman could hardly be mistaken for one another, in the social context of both, we find similarities of function which correspond to somewhat parallel underlying principles of social organization. There are a large number of examples of art works whose scale reflects the power, wealth and particularly the social status of their owners or the people who commissioned them. There is the Taj Mahal, the magnificent white marble mausoleum built by Shah Jehan at Agra in north India for his favorite wife in the 17th century. Reputedly more than 20,000 men spent over 20 years in its construction.

And nearer home Henry III of England rebuilt the east half of Westminster Abbey between 1245 and 1269 at a reputed cost of £50,000 ($125,000), a fabulous sum in those days. He wished, it is said, to be buried there next to his patron saint, Edward the Confessor, in a building comparable in magnificence to Rheims or the Sainte Chapelle. So that when, quite rightly, we designate a cathedral primarily as a religious building, we should nevertheless consider what other functions it has and for what other motives it might have been built. One hesitates to ascribe motives to the artists themselves, particularly to contemporary ones whose work is often hard for many people to understand. But when an artist has achieved a certain degree of fame his works come to be bought and sold as objects of profitable exchange as much as for any artistic merit they might possess. Nor, in a wealth-orientated society, will the possession of a Picasso or two be to the detriment of your prestige with your social peers. Thus in western society as well as in pre-industrial societies, it is misleading to talk of 'art for art's sake'. Whatever the intention of the artist, all art has other functions too. Some critics have seen the aesthetic attitude as the key distinguishing element in a work of art. But it would be almost impossible, in any work of art, to disentangle this from the religious, economic and social elements. Indeed, it would be pointless, for it is precisely these elements – the social roles of art – which in any particular society give it its characteristic forms and meaning.

The art of some 'simple' societies is astoundingly complex. The more one learns about its context, the deeper are the layers of meaning that become apparent. We have seen that effective communication in art depends on conventions shared by the artist and the rest of the community. Conventions should not be seen as restrictions but as the conditions which permit expression, just as the rules of grammar, far from hampering us, allow us to say things. Symbolism is perhaps the richest, most condensed kind of convention, and the hardest to fathom. Artists can abandon 'naturalistic' representation, and communicate by means of motifs which may be incomprehensible to the outsider, but which may carry an immense weight of complex meaning to those for whom they are intended. A double zigzag design on the handle of an ornamental spear belonging to an Asmat man in south-west New Guinea is, to a European onlooker, nothing but a double zigzag design. If, however, he examines more of the Asmat's art – their ancestor posts, the prows of their canoes and their signal horns – he will find the design repeated, with variations, and he may even be able to resolve it into elements which resemble on the one hand a praying mantis and, on the other, a seated human figure with its knees drawn up and its elbows resting on them. Further observation will reveal nothing of the connection between man and mantis. It is only by exploring Asmat culture and mythology that the outsider may discover that wood and headhunting are the common elements which connect the two. For man and wood are closely identified in the Asmat's picture of the world. Wood is their most valuable, and practically their only, natural resource.

The creator carved the first Asmat in wood as statues and then drummed them into life; the mantis is polished and wooden in appearance, with its stick-like limbs which also articulate in a human fashion. The very name Asmat means 'we are trees'. The female mantis bites off the head of the male after copulation; the Asmat were headhunters. All this shows that the Asmat have a special symbolic relation with the mantis. Asmat art is full of such symbolism, all of which illustrates not only mystical relationships between the people, their ancestors, and the creators of their myths, but real social situations too. An Asmat artist can say an awful lot with a zigzag line to those who are in the know.

Our object in this chapter has been to find a way of looking at art that brings out the diversity of its forms and uses and at the same time provides us with a basis by which we can compare art from widely differing communities. One point that emerges very clearly is this: you cannot lump all the art of non-industrial societies together as an undifferentiated mass under the label of 'primitive art' and then make sweeping contrasts with the rich and varied traditions of western art. This is a mistake which arose from the tendency of Europeans to look at the art of simple societies from the outside, in

116

*Inukok*, semblances of men,
limit the infinite space of
the Canadian tundra to prove
that men have passed through
the desolate wastes.

formal terms and with their own cultural preconceptions
as to what art should be like. Inevitably they saw it as
a homogeneous mass which looked bafflingly different
from their own art. Inevitably, even when looking closely
enough to differentiate one people's art from that of
another they were still unable to distinguish internal
differences of style. Consequently they called the art
mechanical, routinized, shackled by convention and
incapable of real expression. What in fact emerges is a
very different picture. Art, we find, has limitless forms
and styles and a truly remarkable variety of purposes.

One of its main purposes is religious. By no means all
art is religious, but a large amount of it is, particularly
in those societies where religion still plays a major part
in social life. For religion is largely concerned with the
uncontrollable aspects of life – death, sickness and
health, good and bad fortune, natural disasters. People
need these incomprehensible things to be explained, and
the forces they believe control them to be made visible,
whether they be ancestors or water spirits, gods or devils
or elemental forces. What art does here is to provide a
means to fix these insubstantial forces in an image; to
give them a location and an identity, real or symbolic,
as a point on which religious attitudes and activities can
focus.

117

(Over page) Perhaps the finest
example of renaissance art is
Michelangelo's ceiling of the
Sistine chapel in Rome. A detail
shows the creation of Adam.

## Islamic/Semitic world

An 11th century sculptured relief above a mosque window in Kubachi. It illustrates the intense love the people of western Turkistan and the Caucasus have for horses and riding.

This wooden door panel was carved in Egypt in the 11th century. The richly developed wood carving of that period often shows animals, in this case horses, in heraldic form surrounded by tendril scrolls.

A minaret rises gracefully from the sea above the town of Al Mukalla in south Yemen.

## Central and northern Asia

The Kalash tribe in Chitral, West Pakistan on the Afghanistan border still carve figures like this horseman, 56 cm high. The Chitral tribes who resisted conversion to Islam made life-size figures for the graves of their dead and kept smaller replicas in the village.

A lamaist deity in serpent form looms menacingly from a temple screen in Ulan Bator, the capital of Mongolia.

A silver disc showing Saint Mamas, patron saint of tax payers, riding on a lion. The style has traces of Hellenistic influence. The disc is only one of many hundreds of examples testifying to the skill of Georgian metal workers of the 6th and 7th centuries.

## Southern Asia

This painted wooden mask, crowned by five cobras, comes from Sri Lanka where it is worn by devil dancers to cure disease.

Richly painted doors of the new royal palace at Katmandu. The swastika, made infamous by the Nazis is in fact an ancient and widespread religious symbol. The word comes from the Sanskrit *svasti,* luck. Similar devices have been found among monumental remains of ancient Mexicans and Peruvians.

Looking remarkably like a medieval European gargoyle, this stone *garuda,* or guardian, scares away evil spirits. It comes from Banteay Srei in Cambodia and was carved in the late 10th or early 11th century.

## Western-dominated world

The delicate tracery of the 13th century north rose window in Notre Dame cathedral uplifts even the most prosaic soul as the Parisian sun shines through the stained glass.

The portrayal of Christ's agony in the garden of Gethsemane was given more power than ever before by El Greco's use of color and his elongated figures.

Western religion has its spirit masks too, for what else is this death mask of Pope John XXIII but a replica of a great holy man after his spirit has left the body.

# Man the artist

This pottery hyena was made by a member of the Shilluk tribe in Nilohi, Sudan. It is 16·3 cm long.

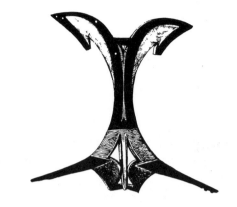

These two stylized birds ornament a spirit canoe used in rituals on Truk in the Caroline Islands. The birds are carved from one piece of wood and are 45 cm high.

This rock painting comes from Nkosasana valley in the Cathedral Peak area of South Africa. It was painted by Bushmen 200 to 500 years ago. Six men, 15 cm tall, are carrying bows, arrows and quivers and sticks surmounted with ostrich feathers, used to drive game.

An aboriginal bark painting from Groote Eylandt, North Territory, Australia. The paint is made from colored earth and applied with a chewed twig brush. The picture shows the passage of a soul after death.

Zulu carving is not usually very adventurous, being confined to simple figures of ancestors. But this carving (62 cm high) is an excellent piece of abstract sculpture.

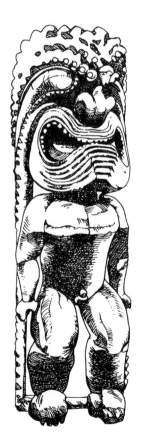

At 208 cm high, this is one of the largest surviving wooden figures from Polynesia. The fierce expression on the face of Kikailimoku, Hawaiian god of war, extends all the way down to his feet.

Amerindia

Orient

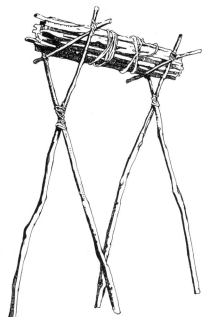

The body of an Igneweter Indian is not buried but is propped on poles high in the Brazilian forest so that the spirit may escape freely into the air.

Peaceful and serene, Buddha looks down upon a saffron robed monk. The temple is at Pusan in South Korea, but it could be in any Asian country for Buddhism has 180 million followers.

Many Indian peoples who are converted to Christianity take on the trappings of their new religion, like this baroque gilded church in La Quiaca in north Argentina. But often many of the old pagan beliefs remain.

Since prehistoric times jade had been more precious to the Chinese even than gold. This *pi* of yellow jade, 15 cm in diameter, was used in religious ceremonies. The perforated disk is a symbol of heaven, an image as universal and meaningful to the Chinese as the cross is to the Christian.

The Kwakiutl Indians of Canada made many masks representing birds, animals, spirits and natural elements which they wore in their dances. This sun mask is made of wood. Each ray is 15 cm long and from top to bottom the mask is 37 cm high.

This pottery vessel, 22.5 cm high, in the form of a mounted warrior comes from Korea and dates from the Silla dynasty of the 5th and 6th centuries. By Chinese standards it is heavy and clumsily modeled but what it lacks in grace it makes up in vitality.

123

(Over page) The Amhara of Ethiopia follow the Coptic Christian faith. They worship in ancient churches like this at Tegre Rock, Abba Salama.

## Islamic/Semitic world

The ancient potters of Kültepe in Turkey often modeled fantastic animal forms. This ritual pouring vase is 20 cm high.

These clay models are toys made by the Tuareg of Abalak, in the Niger Republic. Although they stand only 32 cm high, they are realistic in every way, even to the sense of movement of both camel and rider.

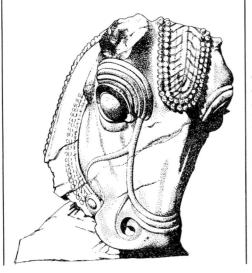

This bull's head is a fragment from the capital of a column which once stood on the veranda of the Hall of a Hundred columns in ancient Persepolis in Persia. The hall was built for Artaxerxes I who ruled from 465 to 425 BC. The fragment is 1.2 meters high but the original capital in the form of a double-headed bull was over 3 meters long.

## Central and northern Asia

Siberian reindeer herding tribes are shamanists. Peoples like the Khanti and Mansi invoke their clan and lineage totems by making sacrifices to their images in sacred birc groves.

Detail from a sculptu decorating the 10th century church at Aghtamar in Armenia The whole section is approximately 1.5 meters high. Accordi to Christian legend, Armenia was the earthly paradise described in the Bibl

A Shaman's charm from the Chukchi peninsula in Siberia. is made of rough wc and consists of miniature ancestral spirits, a bear's head and a cow's head. Each charm is 2.5 cm long.

## Southern Asia

This wooden statue of the Hindu god Shiva stands in a temple in Katmandu. The Hindu pantheon includes some 33 million deities. Supreme above all is Brahman. Next comes the trinity of Brahma the creator, Vishnu the preserver and Shiva the destroyer.

(Left) This seated wooden figure of a man, 70 cm high, comes from the island of Nias off the west coast of Sumatra. On the death of an important man who leaves male descendants a figure is carved. A spider, thought to contain the soul, is caught near the grave and released in the village near the figure. Its soul then enters the image. The wooden ancestor figure on the right is from Leti, an island in the south Moluccas. It is 65 cm high.

## Western-dominated world

English porcelain has become famous for its delicacy and quality. Idealized pastoral figures like this 17.5 cm high country girl with a dog are typical and very popular. Old pieces fetch high prices and are valued by collectors.

This statue commemorating General San Marin's Army of the Andes stands in Mendoza, capital of the province of Mendoza in Argentina. Mendoza was the General's headquarters while he organized an army to liberate Chile from the Spanish. In 1818 a decisive victory established Chile as an independent country.

This elaborately carved snake is the handle of a shepherd's staff. It was carved in the Rodopi Planina mountains of southern Bulgaria in the first half of the 19th century.

127

# Man the artist

Black Africa

Australasia

This female antelope stands 36.5 cm high and is made of iron. It comes from the Karagwe tribe who live on the eastern shores of Lake Tanganyika.

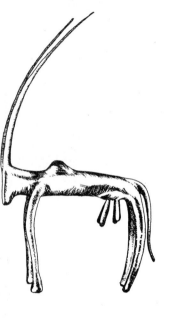

The Bambara, who live around the headwaters of the Niger river in Guinea, believe that a buck antelope was sent by their creator to teach them how to cultivate corn. This carving stands almost one meter high. The Bambara are famous too for their antelope masks.

A cult house decorated with cows heads, stuck into the mud walls. It is in a Kaleri village on the south escarpment of the Jos plateau in Nigeria.

Two water birds car¹ from eucalyptus woo by Australian Aborigines. The sculpture of animals related to the far mo ancient forms origina developed in bark painting. The bird or the left is 57 cm lon and the one on the right is 77 cm long.

These *nggwalndu* represent the major clan spirits of the Abelam who live in New Guinea. The Abelam devote a gre deal of their time to ritual which they believe is essential fo their survival. Young men must pass throu a whole series of ceremonies held on dancing ground of their village. Finally initiates are shown t real *nggwalndu* in th ceremonial house.

This ancestor figure belongs to the Asma of New Guinea. The figure, which is 88 c high, resembles a praying mantis. The mantis has great symbolic meaning fo the Asmat who are headhunters. The female mantis bites the head of the male after mating, and to the Asmat this seem a natural justificatio for the headhunting culture and gives the a special relationship with the insect.

## Amerindia

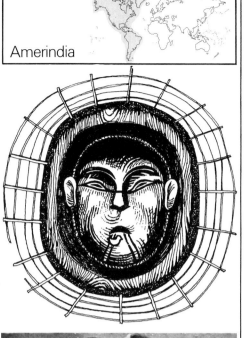

This mask was made by the Unalit Eskimos of the lower Yukon river. The concentric rings around the face show that the mask represents a being from the other world, in this case the woman in the moon. The mask is fastened on with fish skin thongs and the wearer looks through the mouth. The mask is 63 cm high.

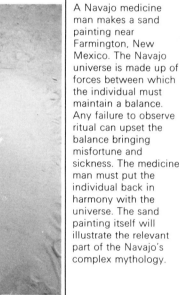

A Navajo medicine man makes a sand painting near Farmington, New Mexico. The Navajo universe is made up of forces between which the individual must maintain a balance. Any failure to observe ritual can upset the balance bringing misfortune and sickness. The medicine man must put the individual back in harmony with the universe. The sand painting itself will illustrate the relevant part of the Navajo's complex mythology.

This *tsantsa*, or shrunken head, was taken by a member of the Jivaro of the Ecuadorian Amazon. It takes six days to prepare a *tsantsa* until it is finally shrunk to about the size of a man's fist.

## Orient

A Nepalese Buddhist painting of the 19th century. In the central mandala stands the eight armed figure of the Bodhisattva Avalokitecvata. This compassionate deity is one of the most highly revered in Nepal. In the middle at the bottom sits the Buddha with other divinities and followers. Three devotees kneel in each corner at the foot of other gods.

The fierce figure of Aizen Myo-O the Japanese Buddhist god of love is made of frozen snow. A great snow festival is held each year in Sapporo. the capital of Japan's north island, Hokkaido.

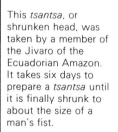

This guardian figure of green and brown glazed pottery was made to stand on a house ridge of the Ming dynasty. It is 80 cm high.

(Over page) Erotic carvings adorn the walls of a Hindu temple near Benares. Vedic scriptures preach that joy is a fundamental part of creation.

## Man the artist

The Nuba of Sudan decorate the mud walls of their houses with paintings. Here the artist is painting a bird, but in matrilineal communities a favorite motif is the breast.

A Byzantine icon of the resurrection. Visual symbols have always been used in the Christian church, partly as a means of instructing the worshippers and partly as statements of divine truths.

Rustem, the Persian Hercules, shot an arrow at his son Suhrab not recognizing him. He was in great despair when he realized his mistake. Today this bas relief 2 meters high decorates the general post office at Shiraz in Iran.

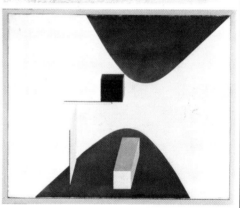

This painting hangs in the Tate Gallery in London. Entitled 'Proun' it was painted by the Russian El Lissitsky in 1919.

A bottle in 'Rhodian' ware dating from the late 16th century. It is 45 cm high. This type of pottery was made in Inznik in Turkey and reached its greatest flowering from the middle of the 16th to the end of the 17th centuries.

A man from Lhasa in Tibet carries a prayer wheel on his way to the temple. A prayer is inscribed on each piece of paper on the wheel and as it turns the prayers are offered up.

## Southern Asia

Daksin-dar (Door of the south), a quasi-god, is identified as the southern provincial governor of the ancient Bengali kingdom. A festival of respect for the deity is held south of Calcutta after the harvest. Afterwards the image serves as a protection against tigers. The white painted terra cotta head is 37 cm high.

Shadow plays based on the two great Hindu epic poems, the Mahabharata and Ramayana, are popular all over south-east Asia. The puppets are made of intricately worked hide and their shapes are projected onto a screen. Performances often last all night. This character, 50 cm high, is Arjuna, a noble knight and hero of both plays.

An image of the Hindu god Jagannath, lord of the universe, (31 cm high). It represents the unfinished form of Vishnu carved from a tree trunk.

## Western-dominated world

Picasso's painting of a weeping woman has a double value — as a work of art and as a valuable object of investment.

This 20 cm high pottery figure comes from Estremoz in Portugal, a town known for the fine consistency of its pottery. The dazzling white outer surface is dipped in red clay and then motifs are incised with a pebble.

The Madonna and Child is a subject which has been continually represented in many ways. This sculpture is by Henry Moore.

133

## Black Africa

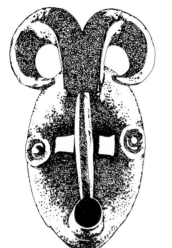

The Ogoni, as the Ibo call them, or Kana as they call themselves, live at the eastern end of the Niger delta. This mask is peculiar to the Ogoni and is used in acrobatic dances called Karikpo. The black color of the 38 cm high wooden mask is due to its storage place between festivals — the smoky roofspace of the hut.

The Tigre monastery at Feeij in Ethiopia.

A wooden ancestor figure from the Bangwa tribe in western Cameroun. A collection of these figures provides the chiefs of the Bangwa with a visible pedigree. This figure is 60 cm high.

## Australasia

This figure of the sea god and creator, Tangaroa, comes from Rarotonga, one of the Cook islands. The god stands 69 cm high.

This female figure with child, 90 cm high, comes from Lake Sentani in northern New Guinea. It was originally placed inside the house, against the house posts or it served to decorate bridges and piers in the village.

The *yanggona* ceremony is a ritual of welcome on Fiji and Tonga. The act of giving *kava*, a drink made from the *yanggona* root signifies the visitor's acceptance into the community; the act of receiving shows the visitor's respect for the community.

Amerindia

Orient

Totem poles are one of the best known aspects of Indian art. Yet they do not in fact represent ancestral or tribal totems. They are more akin to an heraldic crest or to the rancher's brand. They are a sign of prestige, pride in ancestry and rank. These poles are in Kitwancool, British Columbia.

The Ainu of Hokkaido, Japan, are skilled carvers. Unlike the rest of the Japanese, the Ainu are extremely hairy and this accounts for the beard on the wooden figure.

A large pottery vase from the Upper Amazon, Peru. It is almost one meter across at its widest point and 67 cm high.

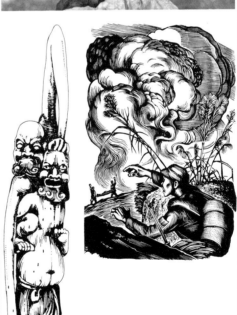

'Comrades, Here's Another' is the title of this woodcut from war time Communist China. It was done by Liu Lun and is 23 by 15 cm in size.

A Kwakiutl killer whale mask from Kingcome Inlet, British Columbia. It is 2 meters long. The fins, tail and jaws are moveable. The killer whale was an important character in north-west coast mythology, generally as a clan ancestor. It was also associated with copper, property disposition and wealth.

Ashinaga (Longlegs) and Tenaga (Longarms) are two of the most famous figures in Japanese legend. They are always seen together, Ashinaga, whose legs measured more than 6 meters, carrying Tenaga whose arms are 10 metres long. They symbolize the mutual assistance that people owe one another in the difficult course of human life. This ivory carving, made in the 17th century is 1.2 meters high.

(Over page) A detail from the roof of the law court in Bali. Prisoners could see that they would be cruelly punished in hell for forgetting ritual.

# Man the artist

## Islamic/Semitic world

Stone lions, 1 meter long from nose to tail, mark the graves of brave Bakhtiari men in Iran. Lions everywhere in the world where they are known, are always symbols of bravery and nobility.

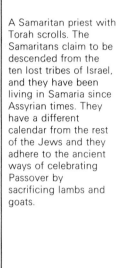

A Samaritan priest with Torah scrolls. The Samaritans claim to be descended from the ten lost tribes of Israel, and they have been living in Samaria since Assyrian times. They have a different calendar from the rest of the Jews and they adhere to the ancient ways of celebrating Passover by sacrificing lambs and goats.

A 16th century Persian miniature showing the return from a raid. It probably comes from the manuscript of works by Sa'di.

## Central and northern Asia

Tiles from the 14th century mausoleum of Ulugh, Sultan Begim i Samarkand.

A portrait of Fandunz, shepherd of Khidzores a village in the Goris region of Armenia, painted in 1961 by Gskhandzhyan, an Armenian painter.

An 18th century Russian porcelain figure of a Cossack. It stands 20 cm high.

## Southern Asia

These ladies of the 5th century painted on the cave walls of the Sigiriya fortress in Sri Lanka, are cloud-maiden attendants of the goddess Tara. The same artists who painted the Ajanta frescoes in India are thought to have done the paintings at Sigiriya. 'Cloud-maidens' is a very free translation of the Sanskrit *Apsaras*, or divine dancing attendants, who see to all the needs of the goddess.

This carved wooden figure, 45 cm high, is from Bali. Most subjects chosen are drawn from the Hindu pantheon. Figures like this were often used as stands for *krisses*, evidence of the deference paid to these weapons.

## Western-dominated world

Pietà by Michelangelo. This sculpture was commissioned between 1496 and 1501 by the French cardinal, Jean Bilhères de Lagraules. It is one of Michelangelo's most elaborately finished works and also one of the most profoundly moving.

A black glazed terracotta figure, 'Sorrowing Christ', made in 1942 by the Polish artist Stanislaw Koziarski.

The Virgin of Mosjö came from a small church in Närke, Sweden. It was probably carved in the middle or late 12th century. The facial expression resembles that of a goddess who holds destiny in her hands, one of the Norns of old legends.

# Man the artist

## Black Africa

The carved hard wood prow of a canoe from the Duala, a coastal people living in Cameroun. It is 2.20 meters long.

A black wooden ancestor figure, 60 cm high, from the Luba of the eastern Congo. The influence of *vidye* is felt throughout Luba country. *Vidye* are the spirits of famous persons, heroes, dead chieftains, ghosts of ordinary men or the spirits of men still alive.

## Australasia

A Maori godstick, 37 cm high, represent the god Hukere. The priest thrust images of this type into the grou before calling on a deity to enter the stick However, the stick its was not ritually effect until it was bound wit braided cord, decorate with feathers and smeared with red och

At Aurukun, Cape Yor in Queensland, men paint wooden carving of crocodiles. The carvings are used in dances re-enacting an ancient legend about the reptiles.

This male figure stand on a fish, 65 cm high, comes from New Irela north of New Guinea. snake is wound round his body, its head und his chin. The man hol a mask with pointed ears in front of his fac of which we see only the mouth and chin. Such masks represent monsters encountered in the forests by hunte

40

Amerindia

Orient

A Noh mask from Japan used in the ancient and lyrical Noh plays.
This character is Hannya, a vengeful ghost.

This bone carving of a spirit canoe comes from the Tlingit Indians of Alaska. It would have been used as a shaman's charm. The canoe is 12.5 cm long.

A bone carving of an Eskimo killing a polar bear. It is 20 cm high.

*Daibutsu* – Great Buddha in Kamakura, Japan. This 13th century bronze figure is nearly 13 meters high.

An Ivory dog's head carved by Eskimo in western Alaska. It is 3 cm long.

Hayagriva, a Mongolian deity, patron of horses which Mongols often value even more than their wives. This wooden carving is 35 cm high.

# Mud telephones and plastic gods: culture contact

In many parts of Africa open markets are made all the more colorful by great stacks of plastic containers and enamelware in every hue. This substitution of products of western technology for traditional pottery is often given as a typical example of how mass-produced objects are inevitably causing a demise in hand crafts in all parts of the world. It is argued that since the hand crafts cannot compete economically with mass-produced goods, they will disappear. In Africa where carved house posts and doors and other craft products were formerly a major source of status and prestige, now cement, two storey dwellings, refrigerators, automobiles and education have become more important status symbols.

It is not really as simple as that however. Western technology is sometimes depicted as a monolithic wave engulfing all in its path. A closer look reveals that there is often an on-going dialogue between the old and the new. While it cannot be denied that western technology and material culture have had a profound effect on traditional societies, the influence is sometimes reciprocal. In addition, traditional societies often put their own stamp on what they incorporate from the technological world – sometimes changing the function for which an object or process was designed and thereby adapting it to their own traditional and particular needs.

As we shall see, cultures selectively and differentially reject, accept and incorporate, often in unexpected ways, the new influences, techniques and products of western technology. To return to our original example, in that open market in Africa, it is not as simple as plastic replacing clay, the new replacing the old. Chances are that large water pots of clay are also on sale, since water keeps cooler in an earthenware container than in a plastic or enamelware one. Similarly, the cement houses may be covered with cement sculpture of traditional and modern subjects in a style consistent in spirit with traditional forms. Societies often retain the best of the old and use the new in their own fashions. The old often co-exists alongside the new.

Fundamentally, there are two ways in which objects of western material culture may be adapted or modified in the process of being incorporated by traditional societies. In one, the function of the object is changed. That is, an object is given a function other than that for which it was originally designed. In the other, the function may remain the same but the form is changed. Sometimes both the function and the form are changed.

There are many examples of the first type of adaptation, where an object is given a new and often unexpected function by a traditional society. This is especially the case in the utilization of discarded items. Men in highland New Guinea have been observed to wear a ballpoint pen through their nose instead of the traditional porcupine quill. They may also wear a piece of a European white dinner plate on their forehead instead of the traditional white shell. Metal Kodak film containers

are often used as decorative items in various parts of the world. In Africa they have been used both as lip plugs and ear plugs. In New Guinea they have also been used as penis sheaths, replacing the traditional gourd. Sardine tins have also been used as penis sheaths in New Guinea. In Africa among the Ibo, World War II gas masks make their appearance in ritual masquerades alongside the traditional wood masks. An interesting example of English words being used as a decorative motif occurs in the near east. The printed information along the selvage of British Terylene cloth, instead of being concealed, is prominently displayed in a panel down the front of the garment. (Arabic script is used traditionally as a decorative device on many types of object.)

In the preceding examples the form remained relatively unmodified while the function was changed. In the case of silk imported into west Africa during the last century, the form was modified but the function remained the same. The Ashanti of Ghana would unravel the silk and use the fibers to weave their traditional narrow loom strips, using age-old designs, to produce the brilliant yellow, red and green *kante* cloth for which they are famous. In the far east, the traditional two-wheeled man-drawn cart, the rickshaw, has been attached to a bicycle and is now called a tri-shaw. Even its new name reflects the nature of the merger it has undergone.

In some cases both the form and the function are changed. For example, in Palestine, the symbol of the hand (said to be Allah's hand), is used as a protective talisman to ward off the evil eye. Where traditionally the hand is made of metal or wood, instances have been recorded where the pink plastic arm of a mass-produced doll has been used instead. In the same area, pips which denote rank on the epaulets of British military uniforms have been seen among traditional status objects such as coins on the headdresses of married women. In these cases, the objects were meaningfully utilized in a manner consistent with the traditional system.

In Australia there are a number of interesting instances of the utilization of imported objects to sustain traditional practices. The metal blades of carpenters' planes have been used to replace the stone blades on the traditional adze. Spear heads have been made of the glass from Coca-Cola bottles. The glass was worked in exactly the same manner as the flint spear heads.

In many parts of the world cast-off automobile tires are used to make the soles of sandals and shoes. This is not limited to the areas of the world where men replace the wheel, since these inexpensive, long-wearing soles are found in Chicago and New York as well as in Lagos and Bangkok. In eastern Nigeria, the rubber inner-tubes of automobile tires have been used to make flapping elephant ears on traditional religious masks. Tin cans are also used by African craftsmen as decorative material on masks. Sometimes the cans are flattened out, cut into strips and affixed. In other cases the ends of the tin cans are used as eyes. Small electric bulbs are also used on masks in place of eyes, an interesting case of analogous function. In many areas of Africa kerosene lanterns made from instant coffee tins are commonplace.

Products of western technology are often translated into other materials by traditional societies for a variety of reasons. For example, they may be reproduced in another material for practical, economic purposes. In west Africa the imported European metal kettle is a common sight. It is not only used for boiling water but is also used by African Muslims to carry water for their religious ablutions which they perform four times a day. Nowadays plastic kettles, often simulating enamelware patterns, are being produced for just this specialized religious function. What at first appears to be a complete functional misunderstanding is, in fact, a perfectly logical, less expensive development when the cultural context is understood.

The effect of certain products of western technology on the religious symbol systems of traditional peoples is one of the most fascinating aspects of the subject. In fact this same imported kettle has become one of the symbols of Islam in west Africa and appears in traditional wood carving, along with Islamic prayer beads, turbans and sandals, as the sign that a Muslim is being depicted. The Yoruba of Nigeria carve wood *gelede* masks for their anti-witchcraft society on which they depict tailors at their sewing machines, hunters with their lanterns and rifles, bicyclists, motorcyclists, automobiles and even airplanes.

The products themselves, such as sewing machines, guns and automobiles, are incorporated into the Yoruba religious system in a very interesting way. These objects, because they are made of metal, have become associated with Ogun, the Yoruba god of iron. Many of the people who use metal, whether traditional iron workers, tailors, hunters or automobile or lorry drivers, become devotees of the god of iron. Certain tools such as pliers and tongs have become the symbols of the god of iron. Consequently, devotees of Ogun, whether hunters or taxi drivers, often carry miniature metal pliers produced by traditional craftsmen in their pockets as magic amulets to prevent misfortune. In fact, when a new sewing machine or automobile is acquired, the new owner may carry out a religious sacrifice in honor of the god of iron, just as a traditional carver might have done when he received a new set of carving tools from the local ironworker. It is not unusual to see new automobiles and lorries parked in front of the vehicle licensing bureau in Lagos with blood and feathers smeared over them as a sign that a chicken has been dutifully sacrificed in honor of Ogun. This practice is, of course, not entirely unlike the practice of christening ships in western culture.

In the Mbari houses of the Ibo of eastern Nigeria –

religious shrines consisting of large mud figures which are constructed over wood armatures – a number of interesting new elements are incorporated. These shrines are usually built in honor of Ala, the earth goddess and may contain as many as a hundred figures, involved in various typical activities. The gods are sometimes shown wearing pith helmets, glasses and wristwatches as status symbols. Alongside traditional scenes such as religious masquerades are more contemporary scenes of tailors at work, of children in their primary school uniforms and of babies being born in modern hospitals, all molded out of mud. Also modeled in mud are the light bulbs and the telephones. Indeed some shrines are reported to have modeled mud telephones in every room which are said to serve as a means of communicating with the earth goddess, Ala. It is possible that the roles of the traditional messenger gods may be partially usurped by more modern means of communication.

The mechanics of the interaction of old and new may be illustrated by taking a particular case study, from the African continent, which demonstrates how modern technology is being utilized by African traditional religion. Twins are held to be very special beings with special powers by the Yoruba of western Nigeria. This is the case whether the twins are living or dead. If a woman has twins she may dance in the market place for alms, singing songs which promise wealth, children and good health to those who honor the twins. Her songs also refer to current political and social events. Islam and Christianity are mentioned in addition to the traditional Yoruba deities. While the songs sung by the mothers of twins flexibly incorporate outside influences and reflect the changing social scene, it is more difficult to see exactly how Christianity and Islam affect the well-known Yoruba wood sculptures – the *ere ibeji*. These images represent deceased twins in the Yoruba traditional religious system. Certainly many Yoruba Muslims and Christians no longer believe in the necessity of twin ritual and in the carving of twin sculptures. They follow the proscription against retaining any images related to traditional Yoruba religious practices. There are, however, a substantial number of Yoruba who profess Islam or Christianity and yet do not completely substitute their new faith for the old. Rather they merge the most meaningful aspects of the old in a syncretic fashion with the new.

For various reasons Yoruba twin beliefs and the images which represent deceased twins have been retained in many instances. In the process they have undergone many fascinating modifications.

Yoruba society age-ranks the twins according to the order in which they were born. This is significant since traditionally property passes through the kinship system according to age, with the oldest child inheriting. The first born of twins, regardless of sex is Taiwo, the second born is Kehinde. However it is Kehinde who is con-

143

sidered to be the elder twin and therefore inherits first. This way of smoothly incorporating twins into the Yoruba social structure is particularly important in the light of the astonishingly high Yoruba twinning rate (45 twin births out of 1,000 which is four times that of the United States and England). During the childhood of the twins, their mother prepares little feasts of beans and other foods for them once a week as well as honoring them annually with a more elaborate ceremony.

If one or both of the twins should die, in infancy or childhood, the small wooden images, *ere ibeji,* are carved to represent them. In a society with a fairly high infant mortality rate for single children, the fear that the twins (who are usually particularly frail) may die in infancy or early childhood is a very realistic one. If one twin dies, the parents commission one image, if both die, they commission a pair. The mother usually decorates the body of the image with camwood powder and the hairdo or hat of the figure with indigo. More recently the brighter blue Reckitts laundry bluing imported from England is substituted for indigo. The sculptures may be bedecked with cowrie shells, formerly the currency of the area, as well as with beads, metal bracelets and anklets. The cowrie shells possibly symbolize the wealth that twins are said to bring. In more recent times, twin sculptures have been observed to wear Nigerian half-pennies instead of cowries, as well as such diverse objects as Virgin Mary medals, plastic measuring spoons and earrings with airplanes and other contemporary subjects. The mother will periodically wash the image, adorn it with cosmetics, clothe it in a little dress or jacket and feed the image on the day when that twin would have been honored had it lived. Images may be placed on the family twin altar, kept in the mother's sleeping room or stored in a container.

The degree to which some Islamic and Christian Yoruba converts still believe in the power of the twins can be seen in some of the new forms which have emerged to represent deceased twins. The typical twin sculpture is about 25 cm high, and consists of a fairly naturalistic, usually unclothed, adult human figure, with arms at its sides, usually touching the hips or legs at some point. Parents of deceased twins sometimes commissioned a simplified form of image because of their faith in Christianity and Islam. In 1930 Christian parents of twins commissioned a sculpture that has the traditional head with all its features but a perfectly cylindrical body. In another case in 1968 a Muslim couple commissioned an image to represent their deceased son and the carver produced a form that was simpler yet, with a round, featureless head and a cylindrical body. The third example consists of a perfectly plain cylinder of wood with nothing to suggest the human form which was commissioned by a Christian woman in 1968 when one of her twins died. In all three cases the parents still felt it necessary to carry out twin

ritual but by asking the carver to modify the image they sought to differentiate themselves from believers in Yoruba traditional religion.

More recently other Islamic and Christian parents have utilized certain modern objects and technical processes to represent their deceased twins. In one town brightly colored plastic dolls which are now manufactured in Nigeria are being used to represent the dead babies. In yet another town an even more notable development has taken place: photographs are being used to represent the twins. It has become the cultural practice there for Muslim and Christian Yoruba to commission photographs instead of sculptures. Each photograph is printed twice to symbolize twinship. The prints are put side by side in a frame and hung on the wall, and a table is then placed under them to bear the weekly food offerings. Photographs have seldom been used as such an active link with the spirit world. Western material culture – in this case the plastic dolls and the photographs – has been used in an institutionalized manner to fill, most ingeniously, a genuine cultural need.

In Africa attempts are now being made to provide African carvers with a new clientele in an effort to revitalize the craft of carving. Artists are being commissioned to make sculptures, reliefs and paintings not only for public buildings such as banks, museums and even petrol stations but for the Christian church as well. An important Nigerian experiment carried out by Father Kevin Carroll tried to encourage the use of Christian images, made by local carvers, in a manner consistent in some ways with traditional religious custom. It is too early to tell whether or not this experiment will take hold.

In West Africa the sewing machine has stimulated the craft of appliqué fabric designs. Among the Ibo of Nigeria appliqué masquerade costumes, formerly made by hand, are now made by machine and are consequently more plentiful. Now, with fewer traditional carvers working, even the face and head covering of the mask are being fashioned in appliqué whereas formerly a carved wood mask was worn. Elaborate masquerade constructions, some as much as 4 meters tall and used for traditional religious purposes, are also made entirely on the sewing machine. The tailors work in a sacred enclosure while they make the structures. In this way the temporary decline of one craft may generate a renaissance in another and modern technology may stimulate certain traditional crafts.

Recently in the United States there has been a return to traditional crafts; in many cases it is a search to find a more personally satisfying life-style. As space exploration pushes back the frontiers in certain areas of man's knowledge, more people seek to explore their relationship to their environment and culture through working with their hands around the world. The dialogue between modern technology and man the craftsman continues.